## DATE DUE

| | | | |
|---|---|---|---|
| | | | |
| | | | |
| | | | |
| | | | |
| | | | |
| | | | |
| | | | |
| | | | |
| | | | |
| | | | |
| | | | |
| | | | |
| | | | |
| | | | |
| | | | |
| | | | |
| | | | |

# TWO LIVES
## *A poem*

# WILLIAM ELLERY LEONARD

# TWO LIVES

## *A poem*

NEW YORK: THE VIKING PRESS
*LONDON: WILLIAM HEINEMANN, LTD.*
MCMXXVI

# MEMORANDUM

*Two Lives* was substantially written in the autumn and early winter of 1913, and privately printed nine years later with considerable omissions. The published version differs from that of 1922 by four scattered verbal changes and by the addition of four new stanzas in Part III.

THE PUBLISHERS

# CONTENTS

Part I.   The White House by the Lake, 1

Part II.   Man and Wife, 35

Part III.   The Green Cottage by the Brook, 71

*Part I*

THE WHITE HOUSE BY THE LAKE

# I

The shining City of my manhood's grief
Is girt by hills and lakes (the lakes are four),
Left by the ice-sheet which from Labrador
Under old suns once carved this land's relief,
Ere wild men came with building and belief
Across the midland swale.   And slope and shore
Still guard the forest pathos of dead lore
With burial mound of many an Indian chief,
And sacred spring.   Around me, Things-to-come
Are rising (by the plans of my compeers)
For art and science, like a wiser Rome
Upon a wiser earth for wiser years.—
Large thoughts, before and after; yet they be
Time's pallid backgrounds to my soul and me.

'Tis no mean city: when I shut my eyes,
To thought she seems memorial as they,
The world's white cities famous far away,
With her own beauty, her own sunset skies
Across her waters, her own enterprise
Beside her woodlands, with her thousand homes,
Her squares and flowering parks, and those two domes
Of Law and Learning, and her bold and wise.
She too shall have, and has even now, her fame
(Like Florence or Geneva, once the fair
Sojourn of worthy men), and of the same
A solemn part, perhaps, shall be that there,
By house and tree, to flesh and blood befell
The things whereof this story is to tell.

## II

I came from years already grim forsooth
With gruelling adventures: as a boy
Puzzling on farmstead my slow way to Troy
With Homer, the Ionian; then, as youth,
Fighting 'gainst poverty to close with Truth,
In colleges by Hudson, Charles, and Rhine;
Climbing in tempest Alp and Apennine;
Drinking with peasants in a tavern booth
By Seine and Tiber to forget a face;
As man, an office drudge for shelter, bread—
My own and others'—with never kind release
From aching eyes; still sleepless in my bed,—
So when Life called me to this lovely place,
I wrote a friend: "I've found my work, my peace."


I found my work:  Life gave to me the lease
Of scholar-shop, as long I'd struggled for,
With desk and bench and blackboard; by the door
A broad blue map of all the Isles of Greece,
Northward to Colchis and the Golden Fleece
And west to Ithaca; beside the clock,
Eternal Parthenon on that high rock;
A plaster bust, the white-helmed Pericles,
In further corner.  Here from day to day,
While through the window flashed the lake and wood,
I taught what Hellas still has soul to say
To generous boys and girdled womanhood.
O had my work remained my all for me,
I had found perhaps my peace . . . 'twas not to be.

I came from other labor, other times,
And other houses, half a fugitive
Till then round earth.   I sought a place to live,
After my needs: a table for my rhymes
And books, a bed for sleep, for human sleep,
A friendly household, that would let me roam
Its grass and porches, like a man at home—
Yet yield (O prose of life!) its roof-tree cheap.
I wandered, hunting, many a pleasant lane
And highway under elms in arching rows,
And many a brick-paved court, with saplings set
And lilacs, rang at many doors in vain,
Whose housewives smiled . . . until, toward day's bright
    close,
I spied a placard: "Attic room to let."

### III

That house stood white . . . with earth's old evening sun
Beside her (yet behind her far and still
Across the shimmering Indian lake and hill),
Vista'd through private oaks.   The lawn did run
In shining emerald, curving like a bow,
(As I explored) O under cherry and peach,
And hedged from neighbors by the goldenglow
And hollyhock, down to a little beach
And rustic shelter.   In front were beds of flowers . . .
Whose names I learned . . . thereafter.   A strange vine
Wound up the pillars with the summer hours,
And two great trunks, festooned with thick woodbine,
Bordered the wooden path—could such a place
(And why?) still crave a stranger's step and face?

Between those festooned trunks, at gable-end
Of that white mansion, looking out upon
The low moon (yellowing after set of sun),
A triple window, like a waiting friend,
Seemed calling me to enter and ascend,
So cosy were the little panes of glass,
Half-curtained in the dusk above the grass;
Joyous it seemed and ready to defend,
As 'twere a living thing, whoever might,
With genial hopes and sinless memories,
Labor by day, or slumber there by night
Within its chamber . . . gloaming fancies these . . .
Then downstairs some one lit an early light . . .
An Old Man pulled the shade behind the trees.

## IV

That attic room became my destiny:
In each man's life there's some excelling spot,
Indoors or out, that may not be forgot,—
Some hall whose music set his spirit free,
Some stream unbridged which lost him victory,
Some hut, some hill, determining his lot,
Dividing still what-is from what-is-not,
In life of each man—whether you or me . . .
Of which hereafter . . . But you shall not think,
You few who read my story shall not say,
"He would make big the things of everyday
By out-worn rhetoric." For my hair is gray
Through manhood's commonplaces, and all ink
Lags ever in the rear of such as they.

That attic room became my destiny.
Although for long elsewhere I've slept since then,
And elsewhere been so busy with the pen
And elsewhere talked, 'tis no mere memory—
For there, still there, I seem to breathe, and be
There, with the spacious light of east and west
From either gable-end, by chair and chest,
Table and bookshelf, looking out to see
Now the still street of elms and now the lake,
As if 'twere windowed only for my sake—
Windowed in front, and yet behind, for one
Who loves on earth, beyond all reason why,
O both the rising and the setting sun,
The morning and the evening of the sky . . .


There by the chimney and the open fire
Of splintered shingles, brush, and billets (borne
In arm from snow-swept woodpile many a morn)—
There, as the yellow flames in tongue and spire
From their foundations leap a span and higher,
And live suspended in the dark recess,
And then, like summoned ghosts in swift distress,
Sweep up the flue, and vanish ere they tire;
There, whilst I lean against my knees, and guess
(Stirring with idle poker now and then)
What song it was the Siren sang to men,
What Helen's girdle, what Calypso's dress,
I hear (for I seem there, forever there)
A tiptoe footstep on the attic stair.

## V

Wild tales of that white house were whispered me
Across the neighbor's fence.  An old dame said:
"A beautiful mother paced, with bended head
And fingers, muttering monotony,
That porch in other days, and seemed to see
Only the squirrels burying nuts and bread,
Which over the rail she tossed them fitfully,—
At last they took her off; her little three
Learned all they knew of her at father's knee,—
And when she died she did not die in bed . . .
She haunts us most when waves are white to view
Under those bluffs"—and pointed down the sky—
"And now the old man is about to die,
And have you seen the old man's daughter?"—"Who?"


"The lovely lone one, the unhappy child,
The gentlewoman, she who keeps the house."
"I have not seen her."—"Like a twilight mouse
She slips away; but like a bird's the wild
Few notes she sings.  Her mother, when she smiled,
Had that same wistful glance—you'll see it there
In the old portrait over the jardinière
Just off the vacant hall.  The father, mild
Of temper sometimes, never free of hand,
Scarce notices her love and her despair
Now in his cumbered age; but sits in chair
And figures rents and dividends and land,
And grudges her the little sums she spends
On orchard, garden flowers, and odds and ends,

That make the house his home." But that same night
Upon my way upstairs, I sat an hour
In library with him. And I found power,
And wisdom, and adventure. Recondite
The verse he quoted by the green lamp-light—
All apropos of journeys over-sea,
Or battles when our armies fought with Lee,
Or foreign politics and civic right.
He had been general, writer, statesman, he
Who owned the fair house now that sheltered me,
And I was proud. And those brave eyes and bright,
Could any "something" be thereunder hid?—
This crown that grief had rendered nobly white!—
I'll not believe it!—(Yet in time I did.)

## VI

He touched not on his daughter . . . But ere long,
One morning passing down, in act to close
The outer door, I heard her at her song.
I listened . . . It grew fainter . . . It arose
Higher within the haunted house somewhere,—
Until, O clear on that September air,
From out my attic window forth it flows—
An old French folksong of the outre-mer. . . .
"So it is she who has been busy there
In household duties with the broom and pans,
And tied my curtains with the new green bows,
And ranged my papers, pillowed me the chair,
And left the plate of fruit, the Astrachans,
And she who on my bookshelf set the rose."

I caught myself that day at thoughts of France,
Humming the folksong that she did begin:
*"The cavalier came riding with a lance*
*And drank the red wine at my father's inn";*
For I had heard it, wandering long ago
Through Savoy in the vale of Chamonix,
Of peasant girl in Alpine afterglow:
*"And in the wars he thinks no more of me."*
Where did she learn it?—So I thought of her
And what they told me.   Beautiful and rare
This unseen presence singing things that were
And serving the stranger with a quick "Beware,
He must not see me," swift to minister
And swift to vanish . . . What was her despair?


I met her first, half-turning up the stair,
Her foot just lifted from the rug in hall.
She stopped, as timid at her father's call.
He introduced me.   She pushed back her hair
With one hand, struggling long to play the host,
Though silent, and, as if afraid to fall,
She clung and leaned against the newel-post
With the other . . . girl-and-woman lithe and tall,
In flowing saffron muslin.   With full throat
And large black lashes over large blue eyes,
A queen of ladies . . . what had she to fear?
And when I thanked her, with an anecdote
And kindly jest, for household courtesies,
She spoke, and almost laughingly drew near.

She took me round the parlor, welcoming:
"This vase shows Ariadne on the isle,
'Twas found on Lemnos. And this peristyle—
(You know it? Notice how the wild flowers cling
About the base.)—I painted one bright spring
At Athens. And that boy in purple tile
We got from Florence. That's my mother's smile,
That portrait—'Mona Lisa wondering'
I call it sometimes." And I startled then—
The fancy seemed bizarre and loveless; yet
She named the name so wistfully and mild.
I looked upon the portrait and again
On her I looked: I never can forget—
In her the likeness of the mother smiled.


"But you'll not find on that piano top"
(She said, as I had turned aside) "what brings
Our house much credit—only simple things
Of Schubert. Father long since had me drop
My foolish lessons . . . O that photograph
Among the music? Do you know him—yes?—
He's married to my sister—O how odd!—
And yet the world is not so big, I guess—
And all are brothers—you believe in God?" . . . .
I knew him. Students had we been together
In Bonn am Rhein, and wandered hills and dells
By Godesberg and round the Drachenfels,
And smoked our German pipes in stormy weather.
And she was glad . . . and called her father in,
As if I'd proved some new-discovered kin.

Surely not so unhappy.   Surely not
So furtive, silent.   Save the moment there
When she had fled me up the broad oak stair,
Cordial to admiration . . . Life its plot
Weaves of all hours, remembered or forgot:
At first she'd stepped aside; then face to face
We did encounter . . . and with change of place.
A cryptic comment?—It was now my lot
To steal from her.   I knew my loneliness,
I knew with sorrow, not with arrogance,
How quickly love might master her and me:
With sorrow, for *I* was crippled by distress,
With sorrow, for *she* had her inheritance,
And marriage was not meant for such as we.


And yet . . . and yet, why should I steal away?
I thought (with wish that hid below the thought
And shaped it cunningly from day to day,
Whilst still what most I would avoid I sought),
Why should we not be friends (she craved a friend),
Why not?   (I too)— such friends, in work and play,
Who know in friendship is their all and end,
And marriage was not meant for such as they.
I knew, of course; of course, she knows, I said;
Safe in myself, I'm safe in her as well:
My warmth will put no notions in her head,
Poor girl, long warned her mother's fate must spell
For her perpetual maidenhood. . . . My guess
I missed with her, dear child—with me, no less.

## VII

Her beauty was upon me.  That alone
Might well have tortured reason from its place:
To look upon that living Titian face,
And the fair Milo's form not now in stone,
And pass . . . when, though but for a little space,
In my young manhood they might be my own!
To look . . . and pass.  I looked . . . and could not pass.
And unto pity for a human lot
Came that great pity Beauty had begot
(The old Vergilian truth) . . . My memory has,
Strangely, half lost her beauty; but there be
Some in the town, less close to her sweet ways,
Who still remark how beautiful was she,
As of some great event of other days.


Her goodness was upon me.  She would be,
As I came in, between maroon portières
And ask me to the parlor unawares
Of afternoons:  "You'll drink a cup of tea?"
And I would follow.  Or with random glee
Surprise me on the lawn, as there I fed
The scampering squirrels scarcely coaxed by bread:
"Here, give them these cracked almonds, and you'll see."
Or knock of evenings:  "Father thought you'd like
This plate of cream—for cream, you know, won't keep—
O I must run and fetch a cloth and spoon". . .
Enough . . . such homely things they strike, they strike,
They pierce me through . . . they come again in sleep . . .
Though (nay, *because*) more dead than earth's dead moon.

. . . . . . . . .

She saw me in blue glasses: "If your eyes
Pain so at night, can't I then try to speak
Your book aloud: I had four years of Greek"—
(Naively as a child)—"and took the prize
As Senior." Was it scholar's enterprise
Made me accept the offer?—For a week
She read me Homer, I with hand on cheek
And temple warding off the lamp side-wise . . .
And watching her. And I'd correct the pitch,
Acute or grave, or chant her the long roll—
Perhaps Odysseus at the bloody ditch,
Talking to brave dead comrades soul by soul;
Perhaps Nausicaa beside the sea,
Or the lone island and Penelope.

. . . . . . . .

I overheard the Old Man  scolding her.
I'm blaming not his anger—peace to him;
Nor probing you the cause, whatever it were
That chafed—whatever oddity or whim—
That you might know her in her sweet desires
And pity her gentle strangeness. Not for this,
Neither on her account nor on her sire's
Do I report.—But for analysis
Of mine own mood and act: I'd have you see
His harsh words through the shut door piercing *me,*
And rousing an instinct that will have its food,
When man approaches woman, as a man—
The soft-fierce instinct of protectorhood—
Spell out my bungled meaning as you can.

.   .   .   .   .   .   .   .   .

And so Life drew us both, and so Love drew
Both, both—the woman without thought at all,
So starved for chance of service all in all,
The man of thought that knew (or deemed he knew).
So reading turned to talk; and talk then grew
To little silences.   Then song grew rife—
The song she most would sing to her was new:
*"Freut euch des Lebens—Take ye joy of life"* . . .
Turning the leaf of music, at her side,
As she ran over the keys, I kissed her hair
One night at last. . . . The Old Man multiplied
And added in his study over there
Across the hall . . . That painted Face so fair
Looked down upon her daughter and—my bride.


"The man of thought that knew."   But came the heart
With sweet proposals, subtle arguments:
"Love will itself create its own events,
And marriage shall become its work of art,—
We shall be strong and happy."   And the word
Of father in the house, of brother, wide
Across the states, confirmed my hope and pride,—
Averring what my pride and hope averred,
And yearned so much to hear.   And so we gave,
The girl and I, with nature's old routine
(Forever new with each new cosmic wave
Of love) our lovers' pledge, unheard, unseen—
And so with lips that played even then the wife:
*"Freut euch des Lebens—Take ye joy of life."*

*"Freut euch des Lebens—Take ye joy of life—*
*Weil noch das Laempchen glueht—whilst the lamp glows—*
*Pfluecket die Rose—pluck, O pluck the rose—*
*Eh' sie verblueht—before it fades"* . . . (my wife!) . . .
*"Man schafft so gern—we plague from morn to morn—*
*Sich Sorg' und Mueh'—ourselves with care and strife—*
*Sucht Dornen auf—we seek too oft the thorn*
*Und findet sie—and find it"* . . . (O my wife!) . . .
*"Und laesst das Veilchen—leave the violet fair—*
*Ach, unbemerkt—unnoticed evermore—*
*Das dort am Wege blueht—that blossoms there*
*Along the roadside"* . . . O'er and o'er and o'er
Ring in my widowed heart the words, the air,
As if I heard them from the Other Shore.


She played the wife, she was the wife indeed
From love's awakening.  In its bird-like joy
Her love was too pervasive to be coy,
Too much the flowering of the native seed,
So long unwatered and unsunned, to need
The tricksy tender teasings that young love
In its first exercise is guilty of;
Too trusting, self-forgetting to take heed
Of any secrets.  But to go with me,
With mushroom basket on a woodland walk,
To serve with many a household ministry
Of pin or needle, and to read, and talk
(As mate already) of my work, or come
Each evening to the door with welcome home,

Was as her breathing.   Nay, she never took
Thought of her beauty.   With unconscious grace
Her auburn ringlets fell across her face,
And her unjeweled fingers held the book.
Her dress was simple as a summer brook
Among the mignonettes, the colors blent
Even as the birds', as if an increment
Of nature from within.   Her voice, her look
Unstudied as the wind, the stars.   Strange, strange,
If I praised her beauty, how she recked not of
My praise, because so happy in my love
As something more, and never stopped to range
One ribbon or give one wandering wisp a shove . . .
Meantime the old smile changed or seemed to change


To utter peace.   And neighbors round about,
The white-haired dames who in the olden days
Had known the mother and her pretty ways,
The humorous gentlemen, so bald and stout,
Who'd call to take the feeble father out
In launch or auto, and her playmates grown
(Now hand in hand with small ones of their own)
Would stop me sometimes, saying: "Who may doubt
What happiness, once coursing through the blood,
Can do for cheek and eye!—It is her food
So long withheld from her by bitter doom"—
(Of this, the half not then I understood)—
"Each day she's richer in her womanhood;
We thank you, friend, we thank you for her bloom."

How I exulted! And the sister, wed
With my remembered comrade of the Rhine,
Wrote from the Tyrol: "O could you divine
How much this touches me!  One born and bred
To live with joy forever, heart and head
Giving to others joy, yet never given—
Her patient gentleness so sorely riven—
But now—but now—she lives—she is not dead—
She lives and *That* can never smite again"—
(Of this, the half I understood not then)—
"To think it should be you!  When we get back,
We'll have so much to talk of.—You've forgot—
But fate has long been busy at the plot:
I saw you once in Bonn—your eyes are black."


But often her father's talk of me she'd tell:
" 'Your beau's a dreamer, better at a verse
Than at a bargain—yet it might be worse:
See that you keep him,—I'm not well, not well . . .
You'll soon be left alone . . . be more the belle
And less his servant . . . you will pall, I say,
Upon him, with your household negligee—
And with your chatter you will break the spell,
And he'll be off.' "  And she would laugh, "Poor man,
He doesn't know you, and he never can."
(He never did.)  But I, between disgust
And wonderment, I did not laugh—in dread
Both of the backgrounds to the things he said,
And of the sweet abandon in her trust.

"This is the red rose, dear, and this the white.
The white rose this, belovèd, this the red:"
As I unpinned the paper, thus I said
In hallway (from the florist's come one night,
When on the square the moon in winter's height
Shone out above Orion) ; and bent my head
With proffering hand, as if a gallant bred
In speech and flowers:   "Be these thy twin delight,
Love's passion and Love's purity" . . . She knew . . .
And kissed me twice—for red, for white, a kiss—
And set in slender vase of gold and blue . . .
In after years I murmured: "This . . . and this" . . .
Opening her box of letters—"Roses?—Two?"— . . .
Each brown and shrunk, a withered chrysalis.

## VIII

One night when early winter had begun
With gusty snows and frosty stars to keep
Our lives still closer, and our love more deep
Than even in autumn wanderings with the sun,
One night when we together, one-and-one,
Were sitting in the cushioned window-space,
Planning some purple flower-beds for the place
After our marriage, with new vines to run
About the basement wall; one night when time
Seemed all to come, and at its coming ours,
And we (as by an irony, sublime
In its gaunt mockery of human powers!)
Drifted at last backward to clime and clime
And years and years of uncompanioned hours,

From  her own lips I learned the awful truth—
Which, like a child of hope with perfect smile,
She babbled, O so innocent of guile—
As some adventure of an alien youth,
Rescued by white sails from a midsea isle
Of shrieking beaks and fins and claws uncouth,
Or eery dream demanding never ruth
Because but dream and vanished the long while—
As something far and strange that I should hear. . . .
And why?  Because she would conceal me naught,
As bound in honor?  No.  Because of fear
I'd learn of others some day?  No.—She thought
Her lover would rejoice—rejoice to share
Her exaltation after *such* despair.


From  her own lips—yes, even as they smiled—
I learned full truth: "In France, five years ago
(When father was ambassador, you know),
*I lived with a band of ladies wan and wild,—*
*Myself a shuddering maniac, exiled*
*With strange physicians, and behind locked door*
*Mumbling in bed, or tracing on the floor,*
*'The Lord is my shepherd, I . . .'* "  "Goodnight, my
    child"—
(That none had told me, seems, you fancy, odd?)—
And so I kissed and left her.  Did I cry?—
I've never cried.  Or did I moan 'My God'?—
Nor that.  Or walk out under starry sky?—
I went upstairs, undressed, put out the light;
And shook with pity and terror all the night.

## IX

All the long night with pity and terror I shook:
With pity for her.  She was so happy; she,
With those blue eyes, found all her life in me;
A thirsting wild thing at a forest brook,
For love was life to her.  If Love forsook,
Again forsook, as thrice in other years,
When thrice her woman's hands reached out in tears,
She'd be, beyond return of laughter, strook—
Forevermore. . . . With terror for self—that too.
Suppose I broke away: to cast ahead
And see that loveliness insane or dead,
And be myself the one who loved and knew.
Suppose, with desperate manhood, I should wed,
What would life give me in the end to do?


Next day I met my classes,—but our theme
Was not the garden of Alcinous,
Nor Hector tossing up the timorous
Boy near the mother, startled at the gleam
Of bristling helmet, nor the flamy dream
Of pregnant Hecuba, nor Helen's fate
To watch the warriors from the Scaean gate,
Nor Agamemnon nor Scamander stream;
Was not of Stoa nor of Academe,
Nor the Ten Thousand's "O the sea, the sea—
Thalassa, Thalassa!"  Not of Greek trireme
At Salamis, nor of Thermopylae—
But of the hereditary Oedipus
And daughter of the House of Tantalus.

I met my classes; at the Club I dined
With colleagues, and our talk was far indeed
From Hellas: of the cell, the wondrous seed
Becoming plant and animal and mind
Unerringly forever after its kind,
In its omnipotence, in flower and weed
And beast and bird and fish, and many a breed
Of man and woman, from all years behind
Building its future.—As I walked away,
I overheard a man of science say:
"Our Grecian here, he needs of me or you
Some caution, if the rumors round be true."—
So much they see whose hearts are not in play,
So much they see—and yet so little too.


There was no choice: convulsed with pain and hope,
I gasped, and then stepped forth in grim repose
Upon the unpathed mountains, with their snows
And green crevasses, without guide or rope
To bear my fortunes up the fearful slope—
Perhaps to perish in the girdling mists,
Mocked by their glimmering golds and amethysts,
Perhaps to reach the sun, and win the scope
Of clear horizons—sometime?  So I stepped,
Not without knowledge, but yet drawn or driven
By powers, stronger than ever to knowledge given,
By powers than all life's wisdom more adept—
And men who'll chide in name of "reason" show
How little they've reasoned and how less they know:

We act in crises not as one who dons
A judge's robe and sits to praise or blame
With walnut gavel, before high window-frame,
Beside a Justice-and-her-scales in bronze;
We act in crises not by pros and cons
Of volumes in brown calfskin still the same;
But, like the birds and beasts from which we came,
By the long trend of character—the *fons,*
*Fons et origo*—fountainhead and source—
Of deeper conduct, whether in unleashed hound
That tears the fleeing stag unto the ground,
Or thrush in battle for its fledgeling's corse,
Or boy who sees the cracked dam, hears a sound,
And down the peopled valley spurs his horse.

## X

And yet my reason still did prop my feet:
"Love that restored her from the undertow,
If still it watches, still shall keep her so"
(If still it watches!).   Or: "Her sister's sweet
Friendship will join with me" (will join with me!).
Or: "From all stress she shall be guarded, she
My gentle wife" (be guarded from all stress!)
"And live the peace of a Tuscan nunnery"
(And live the peace!).   Or: "Love has been no less
New vigor for myself" (new vigor!   yes!).
Or still: "This risk is manhood's challenge—you
From selfish years now rise with work to do,
Of noble service" (noble service!)   —Time
Yields me but mocking echoes . . . and a rhyme.

A rhyme:   this rhyme of echoes low and late,—
But yet another of a louder tone,
Of larger imagery, of earlier date,
"*Amor Triumphans—Love is on the Throne*"—
The title line. . . . A magazine of fame
Purchased the manuscript.  Each month she'd look,
Cutting the pages, in its every nook,
To find the poem and the poet's name . . .
As eager as the author. . . . The delay
Of print is irksome—makes a common jest;
But you who read me, jest not now, I pray—
For that she died not ere she won her quest,
Takes one small item from my grief away—
As you will grant me, when you've read the rest.


But chief of Reason's afterthoughts was this:
"What is it, this mating of the woman-man,
What is it in nature since the twain began
To need the common hearth, the common kiss?—
When are they mated, for the universe?—
When each in other once has found its own,
When each is lost, or all but lost, alone,
Then are they one—for better or for worse.
The ritual, the ring, the surpliced priest,
Concern the civil order and not them;
The flowers, the music, and the wedding feast,
Postponed for friends and neighbors, not for them."—
(True, true; but married life, today at least,
Can not be compassed in an apothegm.)

## XI

Now  each new Warning died with its first voice,
A phantom, a shrill echo, slain at birth
Upon the threshold of the House of Mirth:
For Warnings came, but yet there was no choice;
No choice forevermore!   New Warnings came;
But came too late:   Her dear sweet random ways
Would more and more reveal their tragic phase
(As of a candle with unsteady flame,
Through fierce combustion of uncouth element) —
Proving that love itself, though it can put
Light in the eyeball, swiftness in the foot,
Can not restring, within its choral tent,
The mind 'twould play on (as a lyre or lute),
When God has tampered with the instrument.


New Warnings came: secure in her new life,
She told me of her olden search for death
Thrice thwarted by her father, when with breath
Thrice choked in foamy agony of strife
Under the summer waters off our pier,
Thrice had she felt his hand on matted hair,
Been thrice recalled, as he put forth a hand
Over the gunwale, to love and linger here
Among the living, with love not anywhere—
Thrice in the years ere I had come inland.
Yes, from her story a new Warning came
Of impulse ineradicable and sure:
And Death to her was still a shining lure
(Though hid awhile), as for the moth the flame.

New Warnings came: building the fire, I spied
A crumpled letter with my name, and caught
Some phrases zigzag in the folds, their thought
Leaping into my face:...*"marriage"*...*"have died"*...
*"Avoid those matters and"* . . . *"we're justified"* . . .
So I unfolded (and why not?).   From then
My faith was shaken in two righteous men—
Plotting 'gainst me, yet plotting for my bride,
The sister, daughter.   I was welcome there
As "the solution of her future"—means,
Not manhood, was I unto father, son:
But did they reckon how that deed unfair
Would work across the drama's later scenes
In my own dealings with my lovely one?—


"Yet plotting for my bride":   I think I see
How ran their thought:   "Love and a fixed new goal
Will give her meaning, give her health of soul"
'Twas written; and too near of blood was she
For them to reckon her infirmity
As of the blood, beyond redemption ever;
And I too far, a stranger in endeavor,
For them to take much tender thought of me
And my salvation.   Or was it more than this?
Had they devised, 'gainst what the years might bring,
To shift the burden of her fostering,
And found me, as new guardian, not amiss?—
That Query hung between us like a knife,
Unknown to her, when we were man and wife.

New Warnings came: good friends began to tell
"What some good friends were saying." As for me,
I hushed them by my silence. But to be
(I—deemed a watchman on the citadel
Of Reason once, with cry of "all-is-well")
Now deemed by friends a recreant to the cause
Of living, and of living by life's Laws,
As one now bound and blinded by a spell,
Was hard—and hard . . . and not without a scope
Beyond my pride, touching my work with men,
Imperilling my usefulness, should fate
Some day come calling on the fields of hope
For one best proven by self-regimen,
To speak, as poet-scholar, in the state.


New Warnings came: the children in the street
Or neighbors' yard at tag or prisoner's base,
The babes in go-carts with their mittened feet,
And little necks all bonnetted in lace,
Smiling upon me as I snapped my thumb,
The brides of yester spring-time with slow pace,
And long loose gowns, and God-illumined face,
Bearing within their bodies Life-to-come,
Were still reminders: Love was here on earth
Not only for the lovers. . . . And I seemed
To hear her called to by an infant's voice. . . .
Such were the Warnings in the House of Mirth—
Was I as one who doted as he dreamed?—
I heard, I understood.—There was no choice.

She lacked all analytic to infer,
Knew not my suffering; though afterward,
When things with us began to go so hard,
She felt, she knew what I'd become for her
Or tried to: "O my knight, my rescuer,
From cave and forest, O my savior-prince,
For whom I waited, O long since, long since,
Without your coming, where and whither were
My steps today!"—Her poignant gratitude
Would shame me into silence, into fear—
For on her lashes there would be the tear,
And something not of earth in her wild mood.
And from my neck I would unwind her arms,
And quiet hers and hide my own alarms.

## XII

Of which . . . not yet.   We were to wed in June,
With winter half before and all of spring;
And Love so buoyant in his piloting,
Whistling at helm so cheerily his tune,
Made us forgetful of all far-or-soon,
Made us awhile forgetful of the past
And the irrevocable shadow cast
In sprawling black of quivering rigadoon,
Across the prow.—The dancing shadow black
We marked it not, we three—she, Love, and I—
But there, or with the wind or on the tack,
There with full canvas bulging to the sky,
There, on the waters ever by our prow,
It lay, it lay . . . and I remember now.

Too near to life for poesies, I speak
Not long in metaphors.   Our wintering
Was glorious white and red: white, on the wing
In whirling drifts; white resting week by week
On undulating hills and bluff and peak
Beyond, beyond; white round the house of white—
And white the lake, save where in cirque and streak
The bared ice shone a polished malachite.
The red, the red, the crimson of delight,
Moving across the landscape, set in snow,
And thus more pure, more eloquently bright,
The season's red (O not by nature's freak,
But by her law established long ago)
Was the resplendent crimson of her cheek,


When on the driven dunes we'd pelt each other
(The blue-jays in the bare oaks shrieked their worst),
Romping as merry children, girl and brother
(For Love restores us childhood at the first,
Even whilst it wakes the elemental thirst
That means in time the father and the mother);
When over the bay, more swift than many another,
We skated round the Point to Lindenhurst;
Or, when, returning in her worsted coat
From our "Ice-arrow" (of the winter fleet
Upon the Four Lakes once the swiftest boat),
Outside the vestibule she stamped her feet,
And talked of something warm to drink or eat,
And loosed the fox-furs from around her throat.

Too close to life for poesies, I flout
Most bardic metaphors.   Our only spring
Was red and green—green where the ice went out,
Green in all tints in every greening thing,
And deepening with the northing of the sun
In willow, larch, and poplar, elder, birch,
And oaks and maples, from all greens to one,—
Save for the oriole on his skiey perch,
And yellow crocus, with the earliest thaw
Peeping from out the sodden leaves and straw,
Save for the starry dots of flashing blue
Among the grass, or buds upon the haw,
Save for the cherry blossoms (such as grew
Behind our house), save for the dust and dew.


The red was still the crimson, still as fresh:
The crimson, with her footsteps on the run
Up Willow-Walk; crimson behind the mesh
Of spotted veil, when rowing in wind and sun
Home with wild blood-root and wild maidenhair
(She knew all woodland gullies, every fern),
I watching for our landing, at the stern;
Crimson when lifting her lithe arms in air
To pull a spray of cherry; crimson, again,
As on the rug, spread at the shading oak,
Beside her work-bag, scissors, pins in tray,
And cuttings blown around us now and then
(Across her lap the basted serge and yoke),
She hummed and sewed against her wedding day.

## XIII

Mid-morning of mid-June:  Her sudden whim
Among the guests (who chatted ill at ease):
"O let's be married out beneath the trees—
This mantel with its garlands is so prim."
As if she said, "Let's row an hour or swim";
As if she said, "Let's pick the white sweet pease,
And leave the pink and purple for the bees";
As if she said, "Let's get the shears and trim
The lilac stems." . . . Blue lake and bluer sky
Merged with the green of earth, of odorous earth,
A scarlet tanager went flashing by,
The unseen thrasher sang with all his mirth. . . .
The old dame neighbor said with happy tears:
"The sweetest wedding of my eighty years."


My boat lies waiting where the willow stirs
By cat-tails yonder, moored not now to dock,
Each spruce oar ready in its forky lock,
Well laden for escape (the plan was hers). . . .
We skirt the woodsy hillsides under boughs
That dip in shallows—we grate on sunken stones,
With chuckling speed—we crouch—in whispering tones
We fancy the poor guests scouring bush and house—
We portage over the Neck.  And safe behind
The promontory, with its bluffs and brakes,
Row down the open waters, down the Four Lakes,
From outlet on to outlet, till we find
The hunting lodge, deserted in the June,—
Which was our camp one quarter of the moon.

. . . . . . . .

The long train passed the Great Lakes, on across
The Wheat Belt, over Appalachian hills,
The train with its five hundred hearts and wills
Besides hers, mine, with all their gain and loss
To us as nothing. . . . Back to the old farm,
And father, mother, and New Hampshire pines
I took her, back among the columbines
And granite mountains, ever on my arm,
Questioning ever of my boyhood: "Here
The lane you drove the cows on? . . . This the knoll
Where you read Homer, with no teacher near? . . .
This hollow by the waterfall 'The Bowl'
You wrote of in that love-poem?—What a whirl
Of foam and spray.—What happened to the girl? . . .


"So that's the mountain, that to left of where
The little distant steeple seems to sprout,
From a green world of treetops sticking out,—
So that's the mountain, over the valley there,
You climbed to hear the thunder at your feet—
And all alone,—how could you ever dare?—
And only twelve?—And did your mother care? . . .
O, see the mail-coach lumbering up the street—
You used to drive it sometimes? Let's go down—
I love to see the people of the town
So glad to see you." (And these simple folk,
Though she had neighbored long with Wealth and Pride,
She understood in all they did or spoke—
She understood, because she never tried.)

She knew the ocean but from city docks
Or liner's taffrail—which is not to know;
And thus I took her to the coasts to show
The kelps, maroon and green, the fisher's box
Of brine-sprent tackle, the lighthouse with the flocks
Of silvery gulls around it in the glow,
And the great waters in their ebb and flow
Pounding forever on the mighty rocks. . . .
One sunrise, I remember, as I woke
I missed her; and I followed down a path
Below the cliffs; there off a little beach
I spied her, as the mists about her broke
(Her love and laughter just beyond my reach),
There in the salt-sea billows at her bath.


Once she became the guide, as we turned west,
West to the Four Lakes, the white house: "As June's
The *time,* so there's the *place* for honeymoons,
And we must do in all things as the rest."
(Not often such self-knowledge she confessed,
As jocular critic of the world, but she
Caught now and then some trick of mind from me.)
So at the Falls we stopped. And 'twas her jest
(Type of her own untutored girlish fun),
Wandering the low Three Sister Islands round,
Or watching at Prospect Point in the great sun
The Sun's great waters flash and fall and bound
(I thinking what ten thousand years had done
And, mid my love, yet hearing still their sound);

It was her jest (so like her), 'mongst the gay
Tourists by park and bridge, or at the rail,
With leathern fieldglass in the summer gale,
Besprent with far-flung eddies of wild spray
From round the rainbow rocks of the abyss,
Her jest, beside the eternal cataract,
To cloak her bridehood under word and act
(Secure, when back in chamber, of a kiss):
"Too bad we couldn't bring the children, dear"
(For two old ogling schoolma'ams she said this);
"How worn this bank is since our bridal year
By wave and water" (for mama and miss);
Or tilt herself the scarlet parasol,
And make me let her spread herself the shawl,


Pretending we'd been married long and long. . . .
Was it some subtle feeling that she'd striven
To conjure Time beyond what Time had given,
Or was to give, that suddenly choked my song?—
Or was't that whosoever with keen nerve
Too closely stares upon that charmèd brink,
The gliding shimmer of that green downward curve,
Is wooed from all tomorrows, as to sink
One with the waters? . . . But I broke the spell
Before I plunged . . . said nothing . . . yet 'twas then
Came horror, as to the House of Mirth, again—
As when she told me of her prayer in Hell. . . .
That night we rode into the West-of-men,
To this our city of the Fair-and-well.

*Part II*

MAN AND WIFE

# I

Love's primal want, foreshadowed by Love's quest
Of young seclusion, and, if Love's to thrive,
Proven in practice by all lovers alive,
And by all lovers gone to their long rest
(Beyond the Aegyptian river to the West
No more to love, to linger, and to strive),
Is through the ages not the noisy hive,
But the dear quiet of self-built nest.
She wakes one impulse even as she weans
From others; than herself more great is she,
The Aphrodite of reality,
For her own ends creative of her means:
Through her, mortality forgets to roam,
And plants a tree and stablishes a home.


Why came this need, this impulse, then, with us
To no fulfilment?—which, as unfulfilled,
Grew one long arm of the strangling Dearth that killed
By its embrace at last?  Or if not thus
You understand me, why did we sit there
In that white house, when Love would walk apart?
Why, when already Fear was at Love's heart,
Did I stand forging weapons for Despair
To pierce it with? . . . But I am ill at ease
Coping with symbols in the halls of pain—
As you may mark, confused.  My thoughts are these,
My tortured thoughts in these brief words and plain:
Why, when she needed life with every breath,
Did I thus doom her to that House—of Death?

I did not doom her: for, if clear am I
From rhyme to rhyme, this is a story of
How Time and Circumstance gave birth to love,
How Time and Circumstance did crucify,
With manhood's reason standing helpless by,
Almost to madness. Time and Circumstance
Unto the oak-trees of that haunted manse
Shackled our feet. I did not doom her. Why?—
"And now the Old Man is about to die,"
Neighbors had told me. And new months of life
Made her not less the daughter in the wife
The more his own life lacked for hand and eye:—
A grey head nodding in a pillowed chair
Kept me the husband, her the daughter, there.

## II

Yet, as the captive beaver in a shed
Will gnaw the props, push barrels, boxes, boots,
And build of them (as of the trunks and roots
Of river-trees) his dam, uncouthly spread
From wall to wall, or as the sparrow, bred
In garden aviary, from the straw
Collects some stray whisps for his prison bed,
The fool of nature, working out her law:
So the young wife, with instinct no less deep,
And scarcely more foreseeing, moved and sought
From chamber unto chamber to devise
Within the house which was not hers to keep
(O hers to crown—had life been as it ought!)
Her shifts of happy homing-enterprise.

She tied the curtains all with yellow cords—
Because before they had been hanging free;
She laid green tissue on the pantry boards—
Because all pink before; for home and me
She turned to new bright angles rug and mat;
Exchanged the corners of each couch and chair
And table (save in chamber where we sat
Under the gables up the attic stair,
For from the first she had been busy there);
Reset the vases on each mantel-stone
Of yellow travertin; on shelf she piled
The books anew (her father's, rich and rare);
And hung anew the pictures,—save alone
That where the image of the Mother smiled.


The Old Man grumbled, as with slippered steps
He pattered after her, or as in dream
He sadly chuckled at "the new Regime,"
Quoting fresh tidbits from Montaigne or Pepys
On wives and women and old age. And I
By the stern instinct of man's husbandhood,
Now eager to contract with fame and good
Beyond the home, would sometimes hurry by,
When she would stop me: "Set the flower-pot,
My lady, as you like, on stand or sill,—
But on my head I pray you set it not"—
(And yet that then she laughed is something still).
And sometimes, too, she seemed the restless child,
In her home-making, of vagrant fancies wild.

But bird and beast fail me as honest tropes
In this: they worked in *their* captivity
With alien substance; but my lady, she
Chiefly with what was hers, in old-time hopes
Gathered long since (before I'd crossed the slopes
Of Alleghanies to my destiny),
And cherished long with dreams of love-to-be
Somewhere, some day, with dreams and thwarted hopes
Of home-for-two.—Whatever of slow reward
In silver had been hers from that Old Man
Through years of service, she would count and hoard
For some teak-chest or screen of old Japan,
Some Persian stool and ivory-inlaid board,
Or some dyed basket of the Mexican,


And many a humbler object.  "O for you,
For you I earned, I bought them, every one"
(She'd say when some fresh tidying was done),
"And they were long since yours before I knew" . . .
And once in her own hand a list she drew
(She guessed not why I asked it, in my pain
Trusting her heart, but less and less the brain);
And he, the father, did pronounce it true.
Somewhere I have it still in trunk or chest
(Rather, my mother has it with the rest—
The girlish rhymes she'd tip-toe up the stair
To pin on door in days when love could jest):
In her own hand I have each name writ fair,
With gossip-notes on when she bought and where—

The things are gone.   Odd, how man's brain will share
In woods and metals of insensate earth:
Who rubs the brazen andirons of our hearth
Tonight?   Whose face is in that mirror?   Where
The bed of many slumbers, and the chair
She hung her day-clothes over ere she prayed?—
The cherry dressing table wherein she laid
The silky combings of her chestnut hair?
Whose lingerie and kerchiefs lie tonight
Within the carven chiffonier?   Among
What laughing voices sounds the cuckoo clock?
Whose fingers turn the screw that makes more bright
Our reading lamp—for whom?   Who'll dust the rung
Of the ebon stool tomorrow, or snap the lock


Of her writing desk beside whose window?—gone,
The Things are gone; and I know never whither.
Gone—how?—Because, as being precious *with* her,
*Without* her they became as Hell's own spawn,
Leering my goings out, my comings in,
Like silent demons?—Such they might have been—
And so, as such, to be put by (that dawn
Might find me fearless life's new ends to win).
Did I, then, put them by?—Or did men come
(Whilst I lay helpless in the woods and dumb)
Into that empty house with curtains drawn
(I hear from floor to floor the leathern tread. . . .
I hear in hall the rolling of a bed. . . .)
And pile them for the drayman on the lawn?

### III

True marriage is true love; but love is free
In its blithe exultation, swift to take
Each own hour only for that hour's own sake
Or for its thrill of splendid prophecy.
Today Love walks by mountain, stream, and sea
In Love's own woodlands, wondrously awake,—
But yet Tomorrow may its finger shake:
"Lo, marriage was not meant for such as ye."
True marriage is true love—but more than love
In long, severe, but eloquent, routine;
And spring's brief instinct of the deer and dove
Alone founds little that outlasts the green—
True mates in love, under one law of life,
May, under another, mate not as man and wife.


That maxim we'd discussed and sworn to win
Against its warnings, in no lover's trance. . . .
*"The cavalier came riding with a lance
And drank the red wine at my father's inn"*
She sang of evenings to the mandolin,
*"And to the wars he will not go from me"*
(Altering the old refrain)—and joyously
Each morning tied the apron under chin.
With her the housewife with the love was born—
Twins of her tender, ministering, sweet heart;
Nor was I one who by neglect or scorn
Averred that this was not the better part,
And served not too.—But anxious to defend
Our sacred partnership from grievous end,

Too anxious was I! Hear me, friends, nor blame;
You'll pity her—her in the slumberland—
O pity me? . . . no, no!—but understand
The lonely man who gave the girl his name!
Like to "a candle with unsteady flame
Through fierce combustion of uncouth element"
I said she burned, not only her merriment
Being thus random in device and aim:
For, though a gentlewoman, read in books,
Deep wisdom often in her simple talk
(Deeper than ocean's, fresher than the brook's),
Though deft of finger with needle, flower, or chalk,
Though striving ever with prayer and plan to be
In feeling poised, in conduct firm and free


(Striving so piteously!), she grew as one
Forever apart from all good wives of earth;
'Twas not alone each mood gave impulse birth,
Before a thought could check, in rain or sun;
But thoughts themselves clasped in false unison
How often, quaintly incoordinate;
And memory lapsed both when she walked and sate,
And clock would strike with promised task undone.
Then, too, her vision of life, its lures, its lies,
Its garrulous people stepping to and fro,
Was prismed through her own peculiar eyes
By light which through them from within would flow.
(She lacked—O terrible beauty of her fate—
Uncannily all power to doubt or hate.)

But I, grown fatuous in my love and lore—
Love that I thought was round her as a buoy,
Lore that I thought was cunning to destroy
Disease and doom—toiled with her more and more:
My skill at mind should train the wild away,
The wild and eery, from that brow I kissed,
Till she should grow like girls of everyday
Through me (triumphant lover-alienist!),—
Thus to establish her in selfhood strong
Against disasters I was fearsome of—
Pain, slander, grief, and all gaunt broods of Life,—
Thus, also, to establish her as wife—
As apt in judgment as she was in song,
As fixed in purpose as she was in love.


What issued from that schooling? That I'll write
Brief as the dot-and-dash that spells "He's dead"
Upon the wire for one who waits in dread—
Brief—for at best I shall not sleep tonight:
My watchfulness, too anxious, alert, and sly,
Became suspicion of every act and word,
And many a motion, as natural as a bird,
I tortured to a hint of brain awry.
My lessoning, even where my judgment kept
Its finger on her perilous part, became,
In its long, sad futility, a flame
That chafed, that gnawed me when I waked or slept.
Thus sometimes (name me by the brutal name!)
I chided, I rebuked her—and she wept.

"Striving so piteously":   she hung a slate
Once near the closet (where her kimonos were
And green felt slippers).   That she might not err
From the best conduct of true wife and mate,
That she might grow in strength from date to date
As mistress of the wildness harrying her,
She wrote thereon (for discipline and spur)
Sundry reminders.   But these too showed fate:
In their brief pathos, changed from day to day,
Loving resolves, O often so bizarre,
And self-set tasks of homely 'yea and nay,'
'Thuswise and thus' (which she forgot alway),
They too showed fate and fate not very far,—
And the handwriting on the wall were they.


I found a paper on her chiffonier—
Manila wrapping of a scarf or gloves,—
I read its penciling:   "He says, my love's
More than my tact . . . a child of fifteen year. . . .
He says he wishes I were more like sister. . . .
He says he needs"—and there I saw her stand
In the door, white-plume on head, her shopping in hand,
Smiles on her lips. She came to me. . . . I kissed her. . . .
She marked. . . . Her face fell on my shoulder; so
We clung together.   "I'm so sorry, friend,
You found my scrawl."—"I love you, child."—"I know."—
"Forgive."—" 'Twas for my good—and there's an end."
The rest was silence—the embrace and kiss
Of love with love upon the precipice.

## IV

But such a Moment, leaping from the past
And flashing a dagger now into my breast,
Forces a cry of anguish, which, impressed
On this my page, it may be, shall outlast
My years on earth, and give such Moment power
Beyond its brotherhood of Moments.  Yet
That brotherhood was sixty in each hour
And lived a life that I must not forget—
And live it still.   They hasten to o'ertake
That Moment with the dagger. . . . See, they come
To comfort whilst they torture: here are some
With rose-leaves not yet curled and dried and brown,
Some with fresh cherries, or a plum and plum,
Others are offering verses, others still
Would staunch my wound with laurel from the hill,


Wherewith in jest I once had crowned her.   See,
In bands of Hours, and sixty in each band,
They throng, they lift O each a sunset-hand
That holds a token spray of memory;
They push their sinister companions far;
They beckon me with sweet remindering
In gentle whispers:  "Hear us, we are they
Who saw you patient as the morning star."
Again:  "Hear *us,* for we upon the wing
How often saw you hide your fears away
Under the smiles that gladdened her."   "And *we,*
Saw most of all, saw into silent thought
In  you, and how 'twas she and only she
For whom you planned, for whom you would have wrought."

I thank ye, Moments, visitors of grace,
O how I thank ye!   And ere yet ye fade
Back into Time, whereof your shapes were made,
Give me yet one more look at face and face.
O well ye know the truth—better than these
Sisters behind you, crowding to your place,
Your Sister-Moments of the foul grimace,
Upbraiding Sisters, my Eumenides.
And well ye know, how often, even from her,
From her own strangeness, her my Life-in-love,
From some weird wish, or unforeseen demur
(Were ye not by?—need they be spoken of?)
I lost my labor, able less and less
To help the helpless in my helplessness.

### V

We used to talk, beside the crackling grate
(Between the pages of a Grecian play),
We used to talk so often (after day
Had merged to summer's moonlight low and late),
As she undid her hair, of man and mate
And that one sorrow (bred by love) to come,
When one or other should lie stark and dumb,
With one or other walking desolate.
"Were it not better I were first to go?"
And she would fold me round:  "No, no, O no!"
And though I shuddered, musing the reverse,
Her twofold meaning I was quick to guess:
My love defended her from that dread curse,
And her life counted in the world for less.

The twofold meaning of a woman-child
Whom dread and worship (and humility)
Gave poignant wisdom of the what-might-be:
Often she said, when toward me she smiled
So wistfully on waking and so wild:
"Dearest, could I achieve a selfhood free
And strong with some large aim, then part of me
Might still survive your going."   And, beguiled
A moment by a husband's jest, she'd add,
With hand between the pillow and her cheek:
"How strange that so much love can make one sad;
O, through my knowing you if I could seek
To build your ideal presence that should speak
In widowhood and guard me all I had!"


The twofold meaning of child-womanhood
Whom dread and worship (and humility)
Gave poignant wisdom of the what-might-be:
Often she said, when in self-mocking mood
(That irony of confidence) I stood
Before her, reading some new manuscript,
Mouthing my rolling rhythms, pucker-lipped,
And ending, "Well, my lady, that is good,"
She'd spring from chair, and say, "It is, indeed—
You shall not spoil it by burlesquing so,—
I'll read to you"—And she'd snatch and read. . . .
"How much you've seen of life, how much you know,
And I how little—lead me, dearest, lead;
Being your wife, I want so much to grow."

Her twofold meaning I was quick to guess;
And grimly I record it in my verse:
'My love defended her from that dread curse,
And her life counted in the world for less.'
Touching the first point:   Law, the merciless,
Would, by my death, have broken down the brain
Behind her tears; and whoso thinks me vain
Forgets that Love (which came awhile to bless)
Itself came not to save at last.   But, then,
Touching the second point:   Who knows, who knows
What 'tis to count in divers needs of men?—
I rendered life a rhyme, and she a rose.
I only know, whatever I strive to be,
How much her voice and hands would count for me.

## VI

When she was happy (and unto the last—
So strong is love to battle with distress—
Was she not sometimes happy?—yes, O yes!),
When she was happy, as we watched the vast
Sunset across the lake from lawn or pier
Or summerhouse (through holes in vine and brere),
Or rambled in the orchard till we passed
Knee-deep amid the asters (gardened near),
Neck-deep in goldenglow,—or, as, again,
Returning from the play, we stood at night
Under the full moon (wintering high and bright
In open heaven over hushed homes of men)
Before our glittering roof, she'd say:   "God meant
This house for a poet—and the good God sent."

I've seen the Poets' Houses: Sirmio
Amid its olives where the Garda laves
The ivied ruin still with Lydian waves,
And Casa Magni and its sea below
(Blue Mediterranean in autumnal glow),
And Diodati on Geneva shore,
And the stone house by Ponte Vecchio,
And those Venetian Palaces of yore,
And flowery doorway on the Isle of Wight,
The gables by the Avon's winding mead,
The windows near Winander in the light,
The Gothic Abbey on the river Tweed:—
But by the waters of this earth of flowers
Were none more fit than that white house of ours—


Had it been *ours,* had she been *mine.*— A fate
Ironic, not alone in scope of plot,
But in each tragic detail, shaped my lot,
With cunning masterstroke from date to date.
The poet-scholar walked that fair estate
With love and all the muses, in his prime
For honorable deeds of prose and rhyme,—
Yet poison in each fruit and herb he ate.
Was't not enough that Madness harbored there,
At the house beside the waters (on the wall
In painted smile, and in the perilous stuff
Of Love's own brain whispering of Otherwhere),
And that Old Age was tottering down the hall,
With querulous fingers? Was it not enough?

'Twas not enough, it seems.　O House of Death,
Of Madness, of Old Age, of Love-in-terror,
White house whose fatal beauty flattereth!
I thought 't had been enough—and mine the error
And mine the suffrance with each pulse and breath
In the lone after-years!　"A poet's House,"
Her voice memorial on the night wind saith.
"Nun hoch der Dichter!—bald ist alles aus!"
Say I—so toast me, friends. . . . Am I, too, mad—
By slow infection of that pictured face?
Or have I sucked the taint from Love's red lips,
That thus I rant and ramble?—(If I had,
O only had!—and found with her my place
In that dim Valley of the moon's eclipse!)


No!　Mad?　Not I!　But subtle analyst
Even in my grief, yet for a moment borne
On to sardonic laughter of grim scorn
Against the everlasting Ironist!—
But feel the even blood-beat on my wrist
With your enquiring thumb—am I not calm,
Again as you?　Press on my brow your palm—
Where is the fever?　Smite with knuckled fist
Against my crossed leg at the swinging knee—
My nerves are steady, good neurologist,—
And with firm art's supreme austerity,
I still can draw the face I once had kissed. . . .
Can still report the voice. . . . The tale shall be
Unfolded to the uttermost. . . . Then list:

'Twas not enough: new hands were at the door;
New voices there of tumult or complaint;
New footsteps reckless beat from floor to floor;
New hearts, which cared not if I fall or faint,
Planned the devices of their little world
With scream and song; new fingers hit the keys
To idle music of the dance; unfurled
From room to room new gaudy draperies,
Or mottoed with red letters wall and wall
That spelt out fancies of life's thoughtless spring:
"Be merry, girls! Wissota's got the ball!"—
Or "Don't let Tommy come philandering!"—
Comic?—or ghastly?—taken all in all?—
Death's-head or Harlequin?— They had their fling. . . .


This troupe of college-ladies with blond hair,
This rout of jolly children petulant,
They had their fling, despite all "please," or "shan't"
Of mine or hers; in household of despair
They had their fling with many an "I-don't-care"
And toss of head, young owners of the place—
Each in her girlish chiffon, cloak, and lace,
And velvet hat, bright-plumed and debonaire,
Each with her sweetheart ringing at the bell,
Each with her sweetheart ready for the ball,
Whistling expectantly some campus air. . . .
Strange are the goods that sick old men will sell—
Even to their home, their children, and their all:
And so ye guess how came these ladies there?

And did they rasp the Old Man?   No, not him.
And did the Old Man pity her and me,
Hounded into the corners?   No, not he.
Was it his ears were dull, his eyes were dim
Under those spectacles with golden rim?
Not that.—   But chambers, quite too large for three,
When six times marketed for fee and fee,
Make merry an old heart, put new life in limb
A little while, and naught else matters.   So
The daughter, wife and nurse, from womb insane,
Insane herself of old, and cured in vain,
Husbanded by a man-in-terror (O
Himself well-burdened by past years of pain
That rent albeit they could not wreck the brain),


Became the Matron of the Corridor,
The Keeper of the Bartered Beds—wherein
Her childhood slept and all her childhood's kin—
Yes!—earned her marriage portion, door by door
With mop and broom.   In tears she stamped the floor—
"This, this my bridal year!—The shame, the sin!"
And I?—   O I was busy at the bin
In the cellarage (well coached in honest lore
Of sparing anthracite!)—   "A poet's house"—
"Nun hoch der Dichter!—bald is alles aus!"—
A thrifty old one's clever at a pinch
In spacious chambers, quite too large for three. . . .
(And yet I paid good cash for every inch
Within that house e'er trod by her and me!)

Why did I never flee with her, as Knight
With the Dark Lady from the postern gate
At Flavigny once fled the Sieur le Bête
To cave and cottage after candle-light?—
Why did I never lead her down the path
From that front porch, even though the snow lay deep,
To some 'two rooms with kitchenette and bath'
(Such as we'd looked at), cosy, warm, and cheap?
Or, failing still in this, why did I not
Beseech—and make his suffering child my text?—
I did—I did!  He promised—and forgot:
They left not on the next day or the next.
And his own child for long had loved him so,
Him in the white house, that she *could* not go.


The frolic damsels (whom we served) they knew
Of sorrow little enough; of ours knew none;
The crime upon us not by them 'twas done,
And yet, I think, they will remember too:
Death's outcry on her lips afoam and blue
They will remember even with their fun
In the doomed homestead of my gentle one. . . .
And wish for many a moment to undo.
They will remember, too, as own years bring
The solemn tribulations, how they spread
(So idly flattered, as "knowing everything,"
When town or campus heard her end or read)
Their stories of the cruel husbanding
Of the still husband leaning on his dead.

## VII

I said his child for long had loved him so,
So pitied his desolation, his gray decline.
Though I too tried at pity, I opine,
For her sweet sake, yet forth from this, new woe,
Forth from her pitying love, began to grow:
She would be faithful to her father's line,
And faithful yet to me who called her mine,
Whilst father and husband on her overthrow
Each worked, by rendering her twofold task
Tenfold impossible.   Distracted, torn,
Beside her bed the loving God she'd ask
Each winter evening, and again each morn
(The merciful God upon the great white throne):
"Help me to do my duty to my own."

What was her duty?—   Was't to mix his drink
Whilst mine grew cold—though she did wish it warm?
Was't, then, with "yes, dear father" to conform
When he would have her scour the knobs or sink,
Forgoing our picnic, when (for her own bloom,
For her own song) I begged, "no, no, let be?"—
Was't, then, her duty to build her tomb?—her tomb,
When she should build a home for self and me? . . .
Dear soul of love, between two loves of life,
Two dire contending loves, dear soul, between
The love of daughter and the love of wife,
How wert thou crushed as few have ever been!
Not twofold engine of outrageous hate
Had been so mad, so merciless a fate!

She would please two—two fatal opposites:
Husband and sire, young manhood and old age,
Who had, besides, their fatal heritage—
Distrust and aims diverse. 'Now there he sits
(His ledger in his lap): "Pray, use your wits;
You think too anxiously about him; go
Play with your sister's baby, daughter—so
Leave him to mumble in his moping fits."
(This, as she pleaded for my happiness,
In house of torment and distraction.) There,
O there he sits (his ledger on his knee);
And talks good doctrine how to break or bless
A wildered husband,—which in her despair
Ever and ever she comes and tells to me.


Now here come I (with rhymes half writ and planned):
"He's using us to put himself in purse!—
The dowry? O my child—but that's the curse—
What will all serve him in the shadowland? . . .
Sick?—not too sick to bear us both in hand:
He's using you—you are too good to see
Two hours together! And he used me—me!"
(This tortured sob she did not understand. . . .
Do you?—you do, or will.) So here come I
(With manuscript in fingers) down the stair,
Heedless how suddenly her eyes are dim,
To blame her father with an angry cry—
Which, like a child (his child), in her despair,
Ever and ever she goes and tells to him.

Her end is yonder, certain as the night
Above a stavèd ship with mortal list;
But do you mark, O wise psychologist,
Each cunning means?  Each subtle pang and blight?—
Whereof but one had been enough to smite
The brain of woman in her bridal song,
Had it been bound with bands tenfold more strong
Than the doomed lady's in the House of White;
And yonder my collapse, sure as the abyss
Beneath the broken thigh, the bleeding nail
Of clinging mountaineer; but do you trace
Each ineluctable Antithesis?—
Whereof but one had hurled from off the trail
A manhood tenfold mine in pride of place?

## VIII

Her friends observed her ailing; looked at me
As if to say: 'You made her cheek to glow—
And if it glows no longer, well we know
The reason, sir.'—  That such a look must be
A husband's help in anguish! . . . They gave her of
Fool's counsel for her regimen in food;
And in the corner would she sit abroad
Filled with herself, though selfless in her love.
I hated them for unjust thought of me;
I hated them for folly unto her;
I begged of my belovèd, "let them be"—
And when in her distraction she would err
And seek them out, in my distraction, I
Would fright her, ere I knew it, with a cry.

I feared her friends; but more than them I feared
One who was more than they in speech and power
To smite her suffering goodness every hour;
Yet one to whom, as trusted and endeared
Beyond the rest, the more she clung, the more
The peril now for her—and still she clung,
And I could never thrust him from the door:
*Him?* who?—   Myself, or rather that unstrung
Wreck of my master-self. . . . And night by night
I'd enter in a little book a cross
For every slip in loving—blight by blight—
Until, appalled at loss succeeding loss,
I kneeled with wringing hands and eyeballs hot
Unto that God I knew existed not.


What meanwhile of a child of her, of me,—
Of womb of woman and of loins of man?—
A child of such a stock and born to be
Nurtured in such convulsions?   Did I ban
From out my griefs a child?   And did I save
Some unborn creature, third in that mad line,
Some lovely woman, from an insane grave,
Some blue-eyed daughter that had still been mine?
I did: we had no child, but yet from this,
From this and dread lest on some morrow she
Should witness nature's old fecundity,
Stole morrow by morrow something from her kiss:
Probe life, and know that this and such a dread
Puts a black pall upon a marriage-bed.

What meanwhile of my work for world of men?
What of the Grecian Isles and Marathon,
And phalanx that went forth with Philip's son
To slay dusk hordes beyond the Asian fen?—
What of my solemn midnights with the pen,
The critic's insight and the poet's song?—
Was I at last to be thus thwarted, then,—
I who had struggled for those things so long? . . .
To know my story to the lowest pit,
Circle by circle down to deepest Hell,
Needs must you know Ambition has in it
Meanings that woman's love alone can spell:
Though I said little, she sensed my bondage, she, . . .
And brooded (unbeknown) . . . to set me free.

## IX

Often and often we rowed from off our pier
Out toward the evening star along the glade
That the Wissota sun at setting made
On the smooth waters of that inland mere;
A traveller, still brown from Palestine,
Once told us that for beauty it could be
Likened alone to that of Galilee,
As blue and broad, as ancient and divine.—
"Santa Lucia" rang her voice to me,
"Santa Lucia",—whilst I held the oars
Uplifted with each hand against a knee,—
"Santa Lucia," on the out-of doors. . . .
But over her shoulder often would I see
Upon the bluffs along the wooded shores

Beyond, so far, white turret by white turret,
And a white dome, deep-centered in the trees,
In sunset far-sequestered all, as were it
A magic city of strange destinies. . . .
It was a city: but its gates were banned
With clanging bolts, its streets of ash and thorn;
And there, with wildered eye and waving hand,
A thousand of earth's madmen dwelt, forlorn
Of song and love. There on an earlier day
The Mother (pictured on our walls) would smile,
Whilst her forgotten children were at play
Across the waters wide. . . . And all the while
'Twould seem as if we drifted toward the dome,
And I was nevermore to row her home.

## X

We found him dead one morn between the sheets. . . .
The veterans of his legions came and took;
And there was martial music down the streets,
And at the grave the reading of the Book,—
Unto the earth they gave him with his sword,
With the rent flag of battles south and west;
And his commission (laid across his breast)
Bore name of Lincoln, as his overlord.
So let me leave him: he was old and ill,
And his white house had wrought upon his brain;
So let me leave him, or as hearing still
His talk of Shakespeare even in his pain. . . .
Good night, grim comrade (a deep sleep be thine!),
Whose own wife went the way of mine—of mine. . . .

## XI

The way that mine went soon.   But we have still
Some hours of her young footsteps ere she goes,
Some hours of her blue eyes before they close,
And one more song to hear before men fill
Her grave so near the father's by the hill.
Somewhere amid my papers, when I too
Am gone forever, ye may read them true
(Truer, at least, than verses), if ye will;
But here in casual echoes only: for,
Despite its plangent rhythms, all man's art
At best can but subdue man's life in part,—
Life which, like ocean on a headland shore,
Beats in on peering thought with more and more
And whelms our singing voices. . . . Now that bleak heart


Could beat no more, now the Old Man would call
Her name no longer, were we free at last?—
Perhaps, if this new grief, exchanged for past
(For some past griefs), could yet be made to fall
Quietly from her, ere it seized the brain
With threatening claw. . . . O yes, we should be free:
"Come, gentle sufferer, come, dear love, with me;
Come, and we'll start our love, our life again,
On other shore to east." . . . O yes, O yes!
The haunted house should be our house no more,
And ours no more those waters of distress!
The lakes about our City they were Four—
And one most lovely in its loneliness,
With sunrise, like a prophet, on its shore!

I took her thither on the morrow's dawn:
With backs against our City's westward land,
We stood amid the thickets hand in hand,
Where men as yet had made no walk nor lawn;
From where the Indian beauty seemed withdrawn
Scarcely as yet, and Indian solitude
Seemed on the glittering waters, on the wood,
And on the banded clouds of that Spring dawn.
And then I counted paces left and right
Along the slope: "Look, here between the brush
We'll set our house, facing the morning light,
And waken with the wakening of the thrush"
(The bird that she loved best) . . . She nodded head,
She smiled. . . . "Not so?" . . . "Dear husband, yes,"
    she said.


That afternoon the Postman brought, among
The notes of condolence for father dead,
Our monthly magazine.   I opened, read,
And found at last, at last, the song I'd sung
(Two years before) in print for old and young,
In print at last for every clime and zone—
"*Amor Triumphans— Love is on the Throne*"—
And ran to her with news upon my tongue. . . .
Sitting in parlor, by the jardinière
Under the mother's portrait, with a book:
An instant flashed to life her olden look;
Her olden crimson glowed an instant there;
"Dear husband, thank you."—But upon her knees
Lay the "Alcestis" of Euripides.

Thereafter I found these Greek lines underscored:
"κἄπειτα θάλαμον—*and her chamber then*—" . . .
( . . . O? . . . ) "ἐσπεσοῦσα—*hurrying, hurrying*
        *toward*"— . . .
( . . . So? . . . ) "καὶ λέχος—*and couch*— ἐνταῦθα δὴ—
*Ah, there*— 'δάκρυσε —*she did weep again*"—
( . . . Yes . . . ) "καὶ λέγει τάδε —*and this did say*—
Ὦ λέκτρον —*O bed*— ἔνθα παρθένευ'
ἔλυσ' ἐγὼ κορεύματ' —*where I unbound*
*My virgin girdle*— ἐκ τοῦδ' ἀνδρός —*for*
*This man, my lover*— οὗ θνῄσκω πέρι
*For whose dear sake I die*"— . . . (And here I found
The margin with blurred letters scribbled o'er—
Was it some final message meant for me?) . . .
"χαῖρ' —*O farewell*." . . .        (Dear, χαῖρε evermore!)


That evening, when the plates were cleared away,
I spread on dining table a blank sheet
And drew her near— O near me.  Then, with neat
Pencillings and erasures, and delay
Thoughtful or jesting, planned her, room by room,
The House we were to build:  "Our marriage day,
Dearest, is still before us, and the bloom
Is still to come on lilac, rose, and spray
About new doorsteps . . . see, our study here,
Under the eaves, with window-seat for you;
Here is our kitchen where then first we two
Shall wash and wipe with laughter, no one near;
Here the screened porch for sleep and song and view." . . .
And on her lashes all the while a tear.

When came myself and morning to her bed,
We found her with her hands on counterpane,
Her eyes fixed on the ceiling.   Was it pain?
Or premonition?   Was she dying?   Dead?
She was not dead.— But, husband, lover, friend!
Pour into time, pour into the brief hours,
O self of me, pour all your love, speech, flowers,
And press them to her heart before the end!
O press them close, surround her with your being,
Blot each past slip in loving, quick, O quick!
She still has ears to hear, and eyes for seeing,
Still, still, O man, and she is sick, sick, sick!—
By noon you'll tip-toe from her bedroom door,
And find her never . . . never . . . nevermore.


Lo, had begun again for her the time,
The cyclic time (through Nature's fixed decree),
That woman in her large fecundity
Shares with the barren moon in every clime:
Ten times in the revolving year plus three,
As often as the moon moves round the earth,
Whether a savage, queen, or peasant she,
Then must she pause amid her toil or mirth;
And, as a priestess under holy law,
Pour the Great Mother, pour with reeling brain,
Pour, often with the mystic rites of pain,
Libations of the purple blood of awe,
Blood of no sheep with fillets girdled thrice—
From her own body is the sacrifice.

The Cosmic Rhythms have old right of way,
And roll through man as through the heaving sea:
Should the moon stop above us just for me,
Because I neared the Valley of Death that day?
Should the Great Mother mercifully delay,—
As satiate with ten million women's pine,—
Delay her workings on this one of mine,
Because my wife in grief, in madness lay,
Already stricken?—   Onward still and on
The Cosmic Rhythms roll; I've felt, I've thought,
And I have mated man and star and sun
As of one pulse, one breath, one being wrought,
With gain and loss alike for sun, man, star—
Because ('tis all we know), because they are.


She dressed in white that morning and she passed
So slow, so aimless (*was* she without aim,
Without some purpose that she dared not name?)
From room to room; and now and then she cast
Such piteous love upon me here and there.
I rang my Colleague on the phone to say
"Write on the board, 'my class won't meet to-day' ";
And strove to still my terror and despair
That I might conquer hers.—   All, all was vain,
And turned to dead-sea apples, ashes all,
Or rather into quick-lime in her brain,—
All that I did or said.   She heard my call
Upon the phone . . . 'My work was more than she,'
She thought (and brooded still , , , to set me free).

She heard me say: "Now round the corner, dear,
I'll run an instant to the shop, and you
Must sit and guess what 'tis I'm after, dear,
Or better take this little book-in-blue
(Shelley's "The West Wind," the one book I'd bought her
On her one birthday as a wife), "and learn"
(I spoke as to a little child or daughter)
"At least one stanza well, ere I return" . . .
When I appeared with package in pink tissue
(The playful husband I, with broken heart):
"And now recite, recite before I kiss you
Or open this" . . . "I've only learned a part,"
She answered tremblingly.  "Let's have it, dear"—
"*'Destroyer and preserver,* hear, O hear!'"


"This is the red rose, dear, and this the white,
The white rose this, belovèd, this the red,"
As I unpinned the paper, thus I said;
"Love's passion and Love's purity—ere night
You'll laugh with their green stems amid your hair."
She set in slender vase of blue and gold
(I never saw them after), with slow stare
Put hands upon my shoulders (as of old?—
Not quite), and gazed long and unspeakably. . . .
"These flowers I wore upon my wedding dress." . . .
A pause. . . . "O my poor husband . . . must it be?"
Then clung so close, as in a wilderness. . . .
And then would dart away. . . . "You mustn't go—
Come back; come, sing the cheeriest song you know."

And she obeyed . . . lapsing into the child,
The docile child again . . . upon the stool
Before the music . . . where the mother smiled . . .
To do my bidding like a girl in school.—
And sang the melody of bride and wife,
Thinking of other thoughts she could not speak,—
*"Freut euch des Lebens—take ye joy of life,"*
One stanza only,—and so weak, so weak. . . .
Put hands again on shoulders . . . gazed at me . . .
"I'll sing it only in my wedding dress." . . .
Kissed me. . . . "O my poor husband . . . must it
     be?" . . .
Then clung again as in a wilderness. . . .
Then glided swiftly out and up the stair—
Whilst I sank hopeless in the nearest chair.


An instant—leapt—leapt—followed.— In the hall
I heard the click of key on upper floor—
Strength left my knees— I could but crawl and crawl—
And trembled groping to her chamber door—
I heard the rattling of a box—a knife?—
Razor at throat?—the panel—shall I break?—
Perhaps it's nothing—I grip the knob,—"My wife!
O open! Open for your husband's sake!"—
She opened . . . with a vision on her face,
And hands uplifted to immortal things,
And past me flew . . . upon her toilet case
An emptied glass with foam in awful rings,
And a green bottle labelled with the red
Letters that shrieked upon me, *"She is dead!"*

But in the bath-room, struggling to undo
Her horrible fate, thinking again of sky
And flower and bird, too young, too young to die,
She gulped the antidote my science knew,—
Gulped (as I clapped it in my palm to lip)
In voiceless frenzy—hand on head and hip—
Whilst I repeated: "Tell me, tell me, tell,
You love me, love me, love me!" . . . Then she fell. . . .
The neighbors and the doctors and the maid
Were soon at work beside me. . . . "Is there hope?"
"Perhaps . . . one day will show." . . . My business now
What was it?— In bridal chamber, undismayed
And swift with desperation, there to cope
With love's convulsive hands and sweating brow,


Whilst I undressed her, as she groaned; detail,
The critics tell us, makes reality;
But should I chronicle each look and wail,
Each garment, as I rent it horribly
With twitch and twist of fingers, clutch of hands,
Each ridge in face of me, you'd say I were
(Though doing the waiting doctor's fierce commands)
O not the husband, but the ravisher. . . .
I saw her never after. The next day
The nurse reported from the room above:
"I gave the flowers; she sends her dearest love." . . .
And the next night she heard across the way
My tip-toe in the hall, and wailed my name—
I was forbid to answer: and I came

From out of the darkness not. . . . They led her forth
That morning; I was told she must not see
Her husband now, lest both should blasted be.
They led her to the City west of north—
Across the lake. . . . To die among the mad
Alone, all, all alone . . . next day . . . my wife. . . .
"I'll never see this house again in life,"
She said (I'm told) with the last look she had
Of porch and lilacs, entering the car
With nurse and doctor . . . entering, to die
Alone, all, all alone (and yet not far!)
Among the mad and with no last good-bye,
Entering the auto, murmuring "Where is he?—
Be good  to my poor husband." . . . If•ye be,

Ye that do hear my story, wroth with me
Or puzzled, hear how 'twas they took her there:
That orderly Physician debonaire
Was poorly read in poisons, I divine;
Nor knew how slow their cunning Chemistry
Sometimes may burn before it eats the heart;
Knew not to spell in blood and eye the sign
That yet it burned in her, despite his art;—
And as for me who sleepless stepped and passed,
None counselled aught with me—intruder wan,
Questioning (with scant replies) from dawn to dawn. . . .
*Man blundered with her being to the last.* . . . . .
Alone . . . among   the   mad . . . and . . . "Where   is
    he?—
Be good to my poor husband." . . . If ye be,

Ye that do read these verses, friends with me,
Or friends with Sorrow, as the moment nears,
Now sit with me, without all sobs or tears,
Awaiting, as beside the infinite sea,
On the front steps of that deserted manse,
The ultimatum of the Eternal Deep,
Quiet before the House of Evil Chance,
Whilst she is sinking quietly to sleep. . . .
Hush . . . hush  . . . start not . . . again the phone it
     rings—
One tiptoes swiftly back into the hall:
"Hello? . . . At five? . . . yes . . . so?" . . . Hangs up
     . . . and brings
The word: "She's passed away." And that is all. . . .
Save his good hand upon my shoulder. . . . "Dead? . . .
I think I'll walk around a bit," I said. . . .

When round the open grave the rites were done,
And when the lid was level with the top
(Ye've seen a lowered coffin slowly drop?—
Like to the setting sun behind the plain,
Save that 'tis oblong, black, and very near),
From that small company stept forward one
And laid a burden on the wreathèd bier,
As I shrunk watching in my hopeless pain:
Red rose and white, the manuscript (I mean
*"Amor Triumphans,—Love is on the Throne"*),
And, tied to  flowers and poem, the wedding ring
She'd stripped from finger as she drank the green,
In some wild thought it was no more her own,
As she did that. . . . *O Death where is thy sting!*

*Part III*

# THE GREEN COTTAGE BY THE BROOK

# I

"His wife not dead a month—and there he sits,
Heartless and doubtless happy": so they said
Who at the game between the Gold and Red
Remarked me.— Meantime bases, bats, and mitts,
Pitchers and fielders, flags and fouls and hits
(When up the sky careered the shining ball),
The runners diving in the dust, and all,
Made one blurred nightmare. By my sober wits,
'Twas "most indecorous" that there I sat,
My wife not dead a month!— Did I not know
The use of crepe, the etiquette of woe?—
Yes; but I'd business more severe than that:
Knowing how hungrily Death leered for me,
I seized on life wherever it might be.

# II

Three months with clenched fists and thin bitten lips,
With head thrown back on walks from street to street—
Meaningless highways built for others' feet,
For others' aims—under the silent whips
Of mine own will upon my neck and hips,
Till in the suburbs the midsummer heat
Ripened the roadside corn and fencèd wheat;
Three months of iron-souled companionships
In talks too calm for safety,—till the strain
Cracked to the centre, cracked across the grain
The splintering life of nerve and heart. I fell. . . .
They said that I was dying in the dell
(They said it chiefly who were chiefly fain). . . . . .
O dear green cottage with the windowed ell!

71

Soft midland cottage with the little brook,
In thee indeed had been my place to die—
With the like sound of waters murmuring by
As when in boyhood I would lean and look
At shining minnows darting past a stone;
Under thy eaves, with those who had beguiled
My infant griefs now tending the man prone,
Had been my place to die, again a child:
As one who, having steered by capes and bars,
Seen many cities, warred with many a breast,
Comes, full of fearful memories and scars,
Back to his island and his native rest.—
In thee had been the place, save that I knew
I had this tale to tell, this task to do.


Soft midland cottage of a continent
Betwixt the Golden Gate and Marblehead,
Dear inland cottage whose low roof is pent
Within the hollow where the oaks have shed
Three years for me their old autumnal red,—
Beyond the town, where ridge and roadway hide
All glimpses of the Four Lakes, every side,—
How sorrow has made thee precious as the dead!
Sorrow—and a late-returning mood
That only desperate sorrow can restore,
When the grown man, bereft of all his good,
For those who gave him life must call once more:
O mother, with the wet eyes under hood!
O father with thy white head in the door!

I called; you came . . . from that far mountain stead
Under the Great Stone Face. . . . O granite hill,
And that deep Quiet, sad and patient, bred
Most in the ancient blood of those who till,
How can my angry townsmen look upon
These venerable visitors and still
(Seeing that prophet-beard, that hooded head)
Not see how sorely they belie the son! . . .
Your strength hath passed the Psalmist's farthest year,
But Death hath made alert to death my mind,
And a new shadow grows behind the Shadow—
As in an Autumn sky we see appear
A cloud behind a cloud, above a meadow . . .
And wonder deviously, how far behind.

### III

About my prison-house beyond the wood
(Where first I learned the sheltering grace of trees)
Came visitors to me: the birds and bees,
Sunset and evening star, and all were good.
Came, also, thither three-fold maidenhood,
Three little sisters from across the hill,
Whose innocence was wisdom to my mood,
Whose bloom refuted Death that haunted still.
I loved, I needed them; but Gossips stirred
And whispered, "Let the children come no more;
His brain is touched,"—and so no more they came:
Why, Gossips, feared ye not for bee and bird,
Why not for sun and starlight at my door?—
Nor argued from my love of them the same?

## IV

A friend who'd tramped with miner's kit and gun
Andes and Rockies dwelt beyond my trees,—
A clear-eyed, resolute Australian son
Of England, wanderer of her Seven Seas.
He came how often when the day was done
With handshake, jest, and tale.   (And that was cheer,
And that was honest strength and wisdom, won
Not from the cant of press or pulpiteer.)
But, two years after, even in the May,
They laid him yonder with my wife away;
And it was something to be thankful for
(However solemn in its irony)
That I could come to his young widow's door
And do for her what he had done for me.

## V

Death hath two hands to slay with: with the one
He stabs the loveliness of Yesterday,
Till all its gold and blue is sodden gray
To memory forever, in the sun:
Think ye I think upon our earliest kiss,
Our walks, our vines, our readings, as I would
Were she still by me in her womanhood
To join in tender talk on all of this?
Death hath two hands to slay with: with the other
He stabs the glory of our bright Tomorrow—
Our best reality, our younger brother,
Our spirit-self—upon the fields of sorrow:
Think ye he took no unbuilt house from me,
No unsailed voyage with her across the sea?

## VI

Lone walks and lonelier midnights come to half
Of all who ever loved: that half on whom
Time levies the unchanging tax of doom
For what Time lent us when we used to laugh
In the proud arms of love: that grim remainder,
Heroes of desolation after mirth,
O they are many-numbered on the earth,
And manfully they pay without attainder.
The half that walks no more, that wakes no more,
The many-numbered of the coffined folk,
Know naught, know naught of us, know naught thereof;
And we must bear, with laboring backs and sore,
And broken knees, through life Love's iron yoke—
Without support, without support of Love.

## VII

Some observations touching speech and grief:
After her death of horror, being still
A man of reason with some shreds of will,
I sought among my friends a grim relief
By telling forth, as one who knew in chief,
The story so immediate.  No thrill,
No tears: 'the poison that she drank to kill
Was so and so.'—   Bare fact, you see, and brief.
Three months—and I collapsed—but not in mind;
And in that woodland house imprisonèd,
Too weak to walk, I wrote with bleeding pen
The thousand tender memories left behind—
What I had done for her, what she had said—
In random jottings over and over again.

How little do they know of sorrow, they
Who in the early months of death and dust
In vain commiseration feel they must
Guide their friend's thoughts from what has passed away,
So torturingly fearful lest they say
Aught to remind.— Aught to remind of death!—
As if with every pulse, with every breath,
Death were not talking to him night and day!
But then, when time has led him by the hand
Some kindly footsteps from the grave, and he
Begins at last to look about the land,
Then, witless of the subtle irony,
They name old things and torture him again,
Raking to fire the buried coals in brain.


Thrice summer and autumn passed into the west,
Across her grave with flower and leaf they passed,
Thrice winter with his moon.   Now spring at last—
The fatal spring of her supreme unrest
And ultimate hour—its green young feet hath pressed
Once more on hills and fields and brought to us
From southern oceans small birds amorous
To build in trees of song the happy nest
Above her grave. . . . And meanwhile in the world
Fire, flood, and whirlwind smote the planted ground,
And ships with lights and music sank at sea,
And flags o'er new-born nations were unfurled,
And men discovered, as the earth went round,
New stars off yonder in eternity.

Three years have passed of man's mortality,—
Save for those first strange months, three speechless years,
Speechless (in all things touching her) for me.
But I've debated, mastering agony,
At club, in hall, in household, with my peers,—
The statesmen, scholars, poets, engineers,—
On divers issues: art, society,
Science, and conduct.   I have dried the tears
Of others' children sitting on my knee,
By cutting quaintly with the mother's shears
Lank beasts and yokels.   I have earned my fee
Duly by sundry books men read and quote.
I've dined and jested.   I have cast my vote.


And now on lonely walks by hill and lake
Her phantom clasps my hand; her voice is near:
"O wait a minute! what's the bird we hear?" . . .
"Let's pull this watercress.   I love to make
Crisp salads from the brook." . . . "Come home and rake
The leaves from off the pansy-bed" . . . and fear
Seizes me: for those voices are too dear,
Are still too dear and terrible, and break
The strength I've won.   And yet night after night
(Whatever of else I will to read or write),
The wish to save for others that sweet heart,
Despite the edict of the tomb, despite
The expense of pain for me, with solemn might
Compels me to my record and my art.

But is this self-analysis or—praise?
Am I herein the just interpreter
Of art that follows after things that were?
To save that heart for others and for days
Beyond her bodily span?   That motive weighs
Not scantily, 'tis true; for she was good
And lovely in her girlish womanhood,
And died too soon.   But often man obeys
A subtler self and a compulsion hid;
And I divine that, selfish to the last,
Through this my art I'm seeking unbeknown,
After such long suppression, to be rid
Of what hath worked within me of the past
By making it creatively my own.


But in my explorations of the Dark—
The subterranean springs whence flows the stream
Of speech abroad where men and women gleam,
Clad under sunlight,—gleam and stand and hark,—
Are there no further waters to remark,
No deeper fountain-heads that boil and teem
In the mind's last recesses, as supreme
Perhaps, and life of life, within the Dark?
Yes.   I have found them: Yes, my stream of rhyme
Issues in chief from one volcanic well,
Far, far beneath; and every eddying swell
On-rushing is a sound, far, far from under,
To roll my Vindication unto Time—
Within whose hands is justice and the Thunder.

## VIII

"And do you say, as spokesman of her clan:
'We took you in, we made you one of us,
We gave you freedom of our lake and lea,
Gave you our Loveliest, and you proved no man,
Ingrate and faithless?'—  I will answer thus,
Waiving all question of good faith to me;
Thus will I answer:  'Sir, despite the stress
Of blighted wedlock even to the fatal noon
That most would prove me recreant, she wore
All Life e'er wove for her of happiness,
In love's one year from June almost to June,
And in love's early springtime just before—
The only flowers of joy she ever won
She plucked with him whom ye have turned upon.' "

## IX

'Twas so I wrote her brother, and, 'twas so
I spoke to friends reporting me town-talk.
But by the cottage in the afterglow
Alone, or lonely on a morning walk
Just down the lane, how often have I pressed
Hands 'gainst my temples as to crunch the brain,
How often clutched with gripping fists my breast,
As if to kill heart's pain by other pain;
How often, wakeful on my cottage bed,
How often have I moaned, "And do you live?
And do you know I meant not what I said,
And knew not what I did?  Forgive, forgive!"
And in these rhymes ere now, when pen writ true,
The anguish of remorse has broken through.

I will not fear myself, will not fear truth,
And here shall be arraignment without stint.
I will hold court against my sinful youth,
And all the findings shall be checked in print.
"Item: you fostered a bastard Love-of-fame
Begot on Vanity when still a lad,—
What if you saw that creature going lame?—
What if—when the dear wife was going mad!
What was the peril of Ambition's goal
(Self feeding self, when all is understood),
Against the peril of a human soul,
And that the soul you loved, or said you would?
You have your full reward: the wife is dead—
And your ambition be upon your head.


"Item: you would not meet the issue face
To questioning face: you paltered, eyes astrife
With each mere moment, would not see its place
With years and the enduring laws of life;
And when betimes that Reason which you boast
Did chart some hint of larger meanings there,
Did it, like pilot off a storm-beat coast,
Devise and act to steer you anywhere?
No.   But, astrut, like smug Tragedian,
You mouthed high sentences, and satisfied
Your sense of things-awry, your heart-of-man,
With analytic, passion, gesture, pride.
You have your full reward: the wife is dead—
And all your rhetoric be upon your head.

"Item: not only a bastard Hamlet,—nay,
Arch-Egoist: your triple pride-of-head
(Itself not purest metal) you did lay
On scale, like Troy-weight vilely plugged with lead,
Wherewith the merit of her gold to weigh.
This was your brooding wrath, when all is said:
'I'm being used—I won't be used, I say':
That you, precisely you, should thus be bled—
That galled the most.   And, true or false, that thought
Voided its poison—where!   On her, on her—
The meek and unsuspecting sufferer,
When Love would 'use you' and you had forgot!
You have your full reward: the wife is slain—
And you for her will not be 'used' again.


"Item: for fret and wrath and panic-fear
And sullen mood, too little now it serves
To plead extenuation of sick nerves,
When the remorseless question lies so near:
'Did the sick nerves owe nothing to the fret,
The wrath, the panic-fear, the sullen mood?'
Was there not inward strength and mastery yet,
Save as you sapped it in fool-hardihood—
Until indeed 'twas gone?   Now having known
Collapse indeed, have you not often sighed
(And more than sighed) that energy to own
You squandered in vain outbursts ere she died?
You have your full reward: the wife is dead,
And your fool's folly be upon your head."

Such the arraignment, and I answer not;
My guilt be on my head, without all end.
What thwarts self-knowledge toward my own misthought,
My own misdeeds, is not self-pity, friend,
Nor self-esteem.  But when from roundabout
(Ere one can find himself and his true sin)
Charges and maledictions seek him out,
They so distemper all the man within,
That soon defiance of a base-born lie
Becomes defiance of truth on base-born tongue,
And then defiance of truth, however high,
Of truth itself, though by an angel sung.
Feeling myself less base than some have said,
I've made myself all innocence instead.

## X

Her brother will never know me—he is dead . . .
Her brother in a city far away . . .
A burly surgeon for the Santa Fé,
Who'd swab with iodine a brakeman's head
And clamp the tourniquets on stumps (that bled)
Of scalded engineer . . . along the Trail
Where once (ere round-house, hospital, and rail)
The Pawnee set their poles and bison shed
Their matted wool in spring. . . . But him I saw
Twice only . . . at two burials . . . like a guest
(Wife's picture and return-pass in his vest),
Though I remember a sturdy eye and jaw. . . .
The other, the sister's husband, I knew best,
As then my brother more in love than law.

## XI

I saw him at the club tonight.   He stalked
With lithe step round the table of green baize
Eyeing the balls and cushions, whilst he talked
With his lank partner lightly; then he chalked
His cue atilt.   There's none of us who plays
At billiards more adroitly; so I walked
(In raincoat) nearer, meeting his cool gaze
With silent nod, as one who's never balked
At life's amenities.   He leaned his head
And shoulders, like the physicist he is,
In balance, with long fingers firmly spread
In clever bridge, and that quick arm of his
Behind him like a piston.   Will he miss?—
He made it with deft carom off the red—


A shot I would have bungled. . . . Pondering:
How much, old fellow-student on the Rhine,
Now on this western hill colleague of mine,
And brother once from springtime unto spring,
How much, O you to my imagining
So long my joy in friendship, and a season
My pride in brotherhood, as lord of Reason
Whose fame—(he adds ten counters to his string)—
Honored my low estate, how much you can,
Beyond my skill or glory; you can number
The light-years of the star Aldebaran,
The pounds caloric of a man in slumber,
The electrons clinging to a drop of oil,—
You make the water burn and air to boil.

How much—(he draws with English left and low,
Then runs his fingers through his rich brown hair)—
How much beyond my power: pain and despair
You can so shrewdly bar or overthrow
And go your ways and whistle as you go,
As nevermore can I; and you can trace
My dead wife's beauty on her sister's face,
Without a start as at a demon's blow.
And you can turn tonight the golden key
Of home and hearth, and sleep beside the **Love**
Which most gives courage to mortality
(In this last age with now no God above);
And you, on waking, like a king on throne,
Can call two little children all your own.


And something else you can, because you could,
Brother, because you could and did, my brother.—
(He strikes one match—he never strikes another—
So sure in everything—across the wood
Of amber pipe he lays it, looking down
At flame and puff,—so in old times he stood
With me among the Rhenish ruins brown.)—
O something else you can, because you could
And did, my brother—(Now he blinks toward me,
With handsome beardless face,—these nine long years
Have sculptured not its boyishness away.)—
My brother, my good brother—(Can it be
I've spoken aloud?)—  O guess you how it seres,
Yet seres me?—(No, he is again at play.)—

Yet after forty months of setting moon
And rising sun, and battles with my heart
(That shall be conquered yet!) . . . My shattered part
Of manhood on that awful afternoon,
Prone as an oak-door fallen from its hinge,
For two nights sleepless since she rushed at me
With spumy lips and hands of agony,
Lay, by the doctor's needle and syringe,
In wildered torpor sunken.   Friends stood round,
Rousing (too late!) for journey to her side;
Then you stepped in; I heard a distant sound
As from another planet—'twas when you cried:
"It's good of you to come—but as for him,
I'd let the craven shake in every limb—


Outrageous brute!"   I raised myself in drowse
Half toward you, brother.   You had within your vest
My frantic note of morning:   "My best—my best
I did—I did and lost—this house, this house!"—
I held you up my hand as if for help—
Brother, for help not only that I might
Rise from the blankets.   You grew calm, polite,
And gave me yours; but still my eyes read,   "Whelp,
You're whipped to kennel."   Then (do you recall?),
Whilst staggering round, with wandering fingers back
Upon dishevelled collar, and wandering tongue
Of jests and trifles, I caught you in the hall—
'Twixt living room and kitchen—by the rack
Where my wife's apron and her bonnet hung—

Beckoning the peeping maid.   My guardian sprite—
The deep self under—startled: it divined,
And left an instant even grief behind
In quick defense of my own manhood's right,—
'He shall not meddle in this house of night
And shadow of death!   And that sly thing in tears
Shall with her gossip flatter not his ears
In my own house, and in my own despite!'
Yet when you ordered me away with sneers,
Sneers of cool captaincy of heart and head,
Weak as I was (O brother, how it seres,
Yet seres me!)—drugged, and summoned from my bed
By dying Love, I tottered and I went,—
And you did sound her to your heart's content.


Comrade, the Seven Mountains by the Rhine—
(How much you can that I could never do—
Not only with the red ball and the cue!)—
Still bear on terraced slopes the mellow vine
Whose clusters once were pressed to purple wine
We drank at Godesberg . . . in summer's lure. . . .
Afoot to Bingen . . . *durch das gruene Thal*. . . .
Two voices . . . "*gaudeamus igitur*." . . .
Two voices and one song.   *Es war einmal*. . . .
Afoot to Bingen. . . . Unto you the sun
So many years, my brother, has been bright
That you've long since forgotten his old light
On castle, stream, and friend.—(He makes a run
And whistles to his partner that he's won.)—
But darkness jogs man's memory.— Goodnight.

## XII

I used to think, when over me there crossed
The crookèd shadow of that lonely state
That I foresaw was coming soon or late,
When she I loved should evermore be lost
(For I was reckoning not without the cost—
The sublime debt maturing fast to Fate),
How I could get some comfort at your gate,
O Sister of the months before the frost,
The frost and winter snows.   O sister still
(Because her sister), of your little boys
I dreamed last night in widowed childlessness:
But when this morning on the mid-May hill
You sat beside them, mending them their toys,
You turned your blue eyes from me none the less.


I wrote you, sister, once a pleading line:
"If you've still power to enter the old place,
Though vacant now forever of her face
And voice and footsteps, sister, sister mine,
Then, ere the strangers come dismantling all—
Come whither I can come no more to see
(I feel the silence of our empty hall,
Even in these woodlands, like an agony!)—
O then, search out the broidered silk blue case
(Upon the chiffonier?) and find me there
(The key is in her purse?), under the lace
And scarf and white kid gloves, the lock of hair." . . .
Three years ago I wrote—O lake and hill!
Three years ago—and I am waiting still.

And yet sometimes, I think: Forever, ever,
Not now, and not again, and not again!
Even whilst Death whispered me his "never, never"
Above the gracious wife untimely slain,
'Twas mine, O sister (sister now in vain,
Even should you wish as sister to return?),
To tear your image from my heart and brain,
And lay your ashes in the selfsame urn
With hers forever.   I can name your name
No more than hers forever.   O the cost!—
When two good women (loved the most!) were lost,
The wife, the sister, in one awful flame.
(But O what comfort if as sister, brother,
We might have shared the sorrow with each other!)


Of women the most beautiful, save one;
Save one, the woman of the bluest eye,
And cheek most red and wholesome in the sun.—
(From window would we watch you going by
With babe and husband, once my wife and I,
And raise the frame and call you up the path.)—
Of women all, save one, beloved the best,—
Save one, because, save one, the tenderest—
Before I harvested my aftermath,
After Death's reaping in these fields of life. . . .
And the two sisters used to talk of me
Together, you together with my wife—
Did she not tell me in a burst of glee
Often and often, sitting on my knee?

What flower has been planted on her grave,
I wonder?  By her sister?  Rose or rue?
Who crops the grass?   Or spring the violets blue,
Blue, white, and wilding?   What great branches wave,
The pine or poplar, by the iron fence?—
(Was there a fence?)—  And have you set a stone,
With dates of coming hither, going hence,
And carved a name that ends as ends my own?—
And would you save a place for me thereunder,
Beside her?  (Is the father's grave by hers,
Or by the dear, drowned mother's grave, I wonder?) . . .
O these my rhymes seem uncouth questioners—
When I bethink me 'tis a husband's pen
Has writ them down, whom none will answer then.


## XIII

Yes, none replied to:  "Have you set a stone
And carved the letters 'twas her pride to bear?"
Till strange suspicion gnawed me to the bone,
And in a dream (a dream?) I wandered there,
And saw at dawn a granite block, four-square,
With only her maiden name, and naught to tell
She'd been a wife—the wife who loved so well,
Who claimed in wifehood, thwarted howsoe'er,
Still her Achievement, her Fulfillment! . . . Ye
Who reft your sister thus, in reaving me!
By that sad monument of hate, ye've wrought
Out in the sunrise (do I dream distraught?),
Out in the sunrise, for the world to see,
Something of sadder import than ye thought.

## XIV

I would be just, even as at last I've grown
Kinder in grief to those,—kinder in grief—
In their injustice and unkindness chief—
I would be just, for they too heard her groan,
And they too loved her somewhat as their own,
I will believe . . . and when disasters sweep,
Panic will find the man whereon to heap
Blame and resentment—and deny him bone
Or bread or housing . . . I am schooled . . . and so
In this one stanza that I set below
Read not an accusation; read alone
The witness of its anguish to my love,—
('Twas penned before this book was spoken of
Or planned for friends, three, long, long years ago) . . .
But . . . shall I set it? . . . After all, no . . . no . . .

## XV

I sat in sweater with the college boys,
In crisp October on the sun-bright stand,
Around my arm Wissota's crimson band,—
My arm, with thousands, lifting in the noise
The lettered pennant: down the numbered field,
Down the green field, crossed by the strips of white,
The lines re-formed—Menasha, will she yield?—
Score six to six—two minutes still to play—
Third down—third down—their goal ten yards away!
"Fight—fellows—fight—fight—fight—
We'll win—this—game";—and round their right
Our left-end dashes, and the thing is done.—
Young victors, I was with you on that day
From whistle unto whistle, every one!

O friend and reader, do not think I make
This foot-ball picture for the picture's sake,
Or for some touch of college atmosphere
So poignantly surrounding grief and lake;
Nor that thereby I mainly would portray
How still in the late autumn of the year
I sought distraction with young life at play,
As in the spring I'd watched the batsmen here.
No, but the game, my friend, the fight, the fight!
The message of that exercise of will,
That eager manhood in its unbowed might!—
And, more than message, the resurgent thrill
As, battling with the team, my secret soul
Battled still onward to another goal.

## XVI

I sat unseen in shadowy playhouse; there
I peered and listened, with chin upon my cane:
The footlights lit a world of Souls-in-pain,
And from that woodland world of Otherwhere
Came plangent voices out upon the air
To box and aisle, and beat on many a brain,—
Voices as elemental as the rain,
And deep as earth . . . it was my première.
And when the curtain fell and no one clapped,
And no one rose with hat and cloak from seat,
Though doors were opened, lights were on, I thought:
"Weep there, ye people; I, the handicapped—
The halt, the bent—by art, my art, have brought
This city and her strong ones to my feet."

## XVII

The Club made merry: down the oaken hall
Swept the pied masquers, bounding out and in,
Bending and swaying, to the violin,
To drum and cymbals of our carnival:
Now sprang Mephisto with his scarlet shawl
And slant black eyebrows, clasping Marguerite,
Now Falstaff rolled along with Doll Tearsheet,
Now flung White Nun and broidered Seneschal:
And as I watched alone, from stair below,
Humming the music of the dancers' feet,
Look!—through the flash, the colors, and the din,
Moved a lithe girl, as spotted Pierrot,
With trick of step like *hers,* with smile as sweet . . .
Bosomed against a stripèd Harlequin.

## XVIII

As in old dungeon under marble thrones,
Under old marble floors where walked a queen,
O deeply under in the slime and green—
If that were slime upon those ghastly stones,
If that were green upon the skulls and bones
In vagrom moonlight through the bars revealed—
The courtier beat upon a rusty shield
And sang, to stave off madness, antic tones,
Which wayfarers along the castle steep
Heard as they crossed the shadows of the pines,
And deemed some drunken clown among the wines
In the cellarage, too strange of wit to weep,
And, well remembering his eery laughter,
Mimicked for tavern cronies ever after:

So I from that black pool whereinto Hell
That slew my bride, and Slander, Hell's first-born,
That would have slain the husband (but for scorn—
Which was my strength!) had cast me, there to dwell
Far under Life, the queenly and the well,
Far under Life, to balk my agonies
Thrummed English rhymes from Aristophanes,
Jest upon jest . . . that now friends read or tell
In scholar-evenings by the winter hearth
(Whilst Greek *Birds* twitter to the *Frogs'* refrain);
And I, who walk sometimes in sun again,
Think to myself: "I've multiplied for earth,
Even from the poisoned springs of utter pain,
Somewhat the goodly medicine of mirth."

## XIX

When, midst their panic at our Loveliest
Self-slaughtered near her blossomed cherry tree,
Her kin and neighbors wildly smote at me
As cause and curse, then came my friends and pressed:
"In every house sits Slander as a guest,
And will depart not soon; you can but be
Scorned into isolation in this city,—flee
Forever forth, and leave with time the rest."
To which I said: "For *grief* I might have fled,
For grief and torture of old hill and street
And sunset waters; but, though she be dead,
Her husband's manhood lives on rugged feet
With which he stood on sun-scorched pyramid
And stormy Alps. And here I stay." . . . I did.

I did . . . was't worth the pain? . . . for pain was long,
Long on the cliffs of Slánder; and most bleak
It was to stand so long, when long so weak
With sorrow and the wounds of earlier Wrong.
'Was it worth the pain?— What mattered it what they
Or thought or said? As stranger had I come;
Should I not then, all silently and dumb,
Have, as a stranger, stolen me away?—
Were there no island-haunts by Naples' bay,
Nor yet no mountains off in Thessaly,
No lights in giddy Paris? . . . "Here I stay"—
And it indeed was worth the pain to me:
Not that their slander mattered, but that I
Would prove to self I'd stand my ground or die.


But, as a swimmer, who with head aslant
And left-arm-over, stroke on stroke, hath clave
From upturned craft to rocky isle the wave
Under the scudding clouds, now sits apant
On kelpy stone, and first begins to mark
In retrospect (and meanwhile comes the sun
Along the white-caps) what forces had undone,
Despite his skill, his bounding little bark,
And how: so I bethink me,—being one
(Besides) for whom all suffering at last
Merges with intellect that looks behind,
That is, with reason ravelling the past,
Fibre by tangled fibre, Parcae-spun
And (it may be) by Parcae-hands designed.

So I bethink me: but herein to trace
Lie upon lie from lip to ugly lip
Were a base business for my craftsmanship,
And would but groove new wrinkles on my face;
Suffice the ultimate cause: behold me there,
With all that's life in one lone human heart,
A stranger, as I said, from otherwhere,
A stranger in the hall, the street, the mart;
But she had grown in laughter and in tears
With them in school, by many a garden-bed,
And eaten at many a table many years,
With them who hated me now she was dead.
Yet odd that thus their faith with her they kept—
I was no stranger to the girl they wept.


O odd that thus their faith with her they kept,
To smite upon the heart, the lip, the brow
The man belovèd by the girl they wept—
So odd it challenges my science now:
Shall I, for pity of their tears, accept
This *"ultimate* cause"?—   Not so.   To why-and-how
Of hate that smote the heart, the lip, the brow
I'll answer bravely, as a soul-adept:
Their own remorse engendered that fierce hate—
Suppressed remorse (whose sting they would be spared)
For love and duty scanted, till their fate
Made me their Symbol of a guilt they shared. . . .
Odd too that, though their hate I may contemn,
In *my* remorse I've felt no hate for them. . . .

"I've found my work, my peace."   'Twas thus I'd written
The dearest friend, when first beneath these skies:
How far I found "my peace" ye do surmise;
But "work" remained, salvation for the Smitten.
O Work, bear witness how to thee I gasped,
As hope and God.   Judge, Workers, what it meant
When *that* was threatened, as its hand I clasped
Once more at length.   For Slander's argument
Lurked even by the Campus Hall and stole
The ear and tongue and what there was of soul
In him my quondam Chief.   But yet not thus. . . .
And I survive him here . . . and seasons roll. . . .
So with my classes still do I discuss
With point "Prometheus Bound" of Aeschylus!


Yes . . . "οὐδέ μοι ποταίνιον —to me
*No unfamiliar face can Sorrow wear"*—
And truly "τὴν πεπρωμένην δὲ χρὴ
αἶσαν φέρειν —'tis ever mine to bear
Ordainèd fate— ὡς ῥᾶστα —as I may"*—
(O wise Prometheus!)— "γιγνώσκονθ᾽ ὅτι"—
(O strong Prometheus!)—"*well, O well aware*—
τὸ τῆς ἀνάγκης —*that Necessity"*—
(Grim hero!)— "ἔστ᾽ ἀδήριτον σθένος—
*Is the unbattled might"*— (Rock-chained-for-aye,
Thou knew'st!)— "ἀλλ᾽ οὔτε σιγᾶν οὔτε μὴ
σιγᾶν τύχας —*but how such lot and loss*
*To tell or not to tell"*—(thou Face divine!)—
οἷόν τέ μοι τάσδ᾽ ἐστί —*as is mine!"*

## XX

And nights, in study-den, in windowed ell,
While father and mother slept, I've read below
(Friends with the fire-flies outside or . . . snow)
In Faust, Euripides, and Dante's Hell:
For none but the strongest have a word to tell;
And, with mind quickened by a master-woe,
I know with Shakespeare (some can never know)
The organ and violin from silver bell
And willow-whistle. . . . Yes, the strongest make
Their music out of thinking and heart-break. . . .
O dear Alcestis, Gretchen, Beatricë,
O wife with these . . . *nessun maggior dolore*
*Che ricordarsi del tempo felice*
*Nella miseria* . . . how old my story. . . .

## XXI

And yet all this were challenge to be strong,
And exercise of valor, for high days
That lie beyond the mountains of dispraise
And torture: but to this, a monstrous Wrong
Comes, with its demon tentacles, along
And clutches me forever, and divides
(And O how easy were all ills besides!)
My soul from courage and my lips from song.
This Wrong is Terror.  Ye have heard the name;
Ye never knew the thing:  It has no cave
Under the night-hills or the yellow wave,
Nor dwells not in the earthquake or the flame.
No, no, within my breast, it feeds, it sleeps;
And when 'tis plenished, forth it leaps, it leaps.

Let me enlighten. 'Tis no metaphor—
My poet-youth is gone with all the foam
And spindrift of the seas I used to roam.
Let me enlighten. Deep within the core
Of consciousness there lurks forevermore
In man Primeval Fear, a heritage
From pricked-up Ears and scurrying Feet in age
Of olden alien beasts of cliff and shore.
It lurks unknown, but let man's mind (so free,
So full of gracious fancies, hopes, and jest
In this the quiet latter world) once be
Jarred to the center,'twill rise manifest;
And take by thousands phobic shape and twist—
Unexorcised by tongue, or eye, or fist.


Yet it forewarns you all. If once ye'll con
With inward-peering eye your house of mind,
Mastering unscathed the Gnothi Seauton,
Some shivery bugaboo each one shall find
In corner where the lights burn blue and thick.
For now at this, and now at that ye shy,
With secret shame, ye folk, unknowing why,
And call your perturbation, "notion," "trick":
Some dread all cats or dogs, and some a crowd,
Some dread lest foolishly they scream aloud,
Some dread a knife, a tower, a waterfall;—
Small Pesterings of thought that come and go—
Yet spawned by Her, the Aboriginal,
The Terror that I tell you lurks below.

What is it like (you ask perplexed), this fear?—
Fancy yourself compelled to walk a plank
From cliff to lofty cliff with reeling shank;
Fancy yourself a swimmer, in the rear
Of some white ship that nevermore draws near;
Fancy yourself entangled in the dank
Morasses, with the elephants that sank,
As sole companions, save the moon's half-sphere—
'Tis like such times.   The safe bright world of tree
And dell and house is round me where I roam,
But so estranged, through what's estranged in me,
That it seems horribly no more my home. . . .
In mood, the lost, the panic-stricken child;
In intellect, the man, from joy exiled.


But Terror's widened bane has been to me
More than all terror, whispering at my right
Whispers of *her* by day, and O by night
Close at my left whispering so fearfully
The story of *her* anguish.   An iron key
Did Terror force into my hand, whereby
Perforce I did unlock for mine own eye
The torture-chambers of the mind where *she*
In her last months lay prone.   And *my* strange spells
Became interpretation of the Hells
That *she* had suffered; and I suffered thus
(And sometimes still) her suffering with my own,
Suffered her suffering even as *she* lay prone
In those last months.   And still do I discuss

At times with self (when self is gripped anew
By Terror and its imps of ghoulish play):
"Is there not fate in this?—   Must I not too,
Now knowing in *myself* what *she* went through,
End, when my hour is come, the self-same way?"—
And that Suggestion is of voice and hue,
Of hollowest voice and most unearthly hue
And chief of Terrors, every first of May.
Yet Reason smiles and answers: "Twixt ye twain,
Though *one* by love and later *one* by pain,
The bonds of fate are loosened:  Neither could,
Nor love nor suffering, make ye one in brain;
For in *her* spirit was my speech in vain,
In *yours* it watches every alien mood."

## XXII

My father and my mother tell me:  "Son,
Our life is your life, for we live through you"
(Thinking . . . at peace . . . how little they had done
Of all the larger things they'd hoped to do);
My father and my mother tell me too:
"She was the gentlest and the loveliest one. . . ."
And they had kissed her, red in bridal blue,
Stepping from the mail-coach, in the mountain sun. . . .
Ye guard my hope, ye know my memories;
Yet such the estrangements wrought in me by pain,
Ye merge with the comfort of dumb crags and trees
(That echo an outcry muffled by the rain) . . .
Or ye torture with reminders, when ye call,
Of childhood . . . and what might have been for all. . . .

## XXIII

Opening a Bible, some old text to scan
For use in lecture, I discovered there
Her faded picture and a lock of hair
Hidden away by that strange dead Old Man,
Her father. . . . I went on as I began,
And found the text . . . and laid the black book down. . . .
It was an untouched proof . . . I think . . . and brown . . .
The bust still clear . . . and the same smilings ran
From lips and eyes. . . . When she was laid away,
I gave my mother all of hers I had,
To hide from me her love-notes and her face,—
And this intruding instant shook Today,
For all its sunlight and the west wind glad
Across the Four Lakes, to its utter base.

## XXIV

This afternoon on Willow-Walk alone
I wandered from my desk and books away:
The crew was in the shell upon the bay,
Eight slanting backs, the coach with megaphone
Aft in his launch; a girl upon a roan
Went cantering by me, with a cherry-spray
For riding whip. . . . Three years ago today. . . .
Still clings the flesh in coffin to the bone?
Then, as I gazed across the flashing May,
Strangely I yearned again to boyhood hills,
Where, sitting on the sagging pasture bars,
I'd watch the moon on windrows of the hay,
And whistle to the answering whippoorwills,
And wonder at the history of the stars.

## XXV

By mocking influence of those buried tears
That burned beneath my lids and never flowed,
Whose dry heat parched my eyes for three long years,
I stand, a beggar on the thronging road,
And ask an alms of Happiness, the King,
Who passes with his giddy retinue. . . .
As if in self-protection well he knew
My beggar's blessing were a dangerous thing,
Fraught with inveterate irony; or saw
Such premature sad wisdom in my face,
As touched his merry heart with sudden awe
Of taint prophetic in his royal race,—
Or marked me as a Stranger in the Land,
Speaking a tongue he could not understand.

## XXVI

What is it like, to be as I have been
In these my times of darkness and lone song?
You ask, but will not tarry over-long
For answer, having friends of gayer mien
And business more akin? Well, let me find
Some old adventure that with brief and swift
Symbols may suddenly supply the gift
Of vision for you.— Yes, there comes to mind
From my own later boyhood, strong and free,
An alien hour of sombre mystery
Among Bavarian mountains,—short to tell,—
Of all my hours at home or over-sea,
That which was fullest of great prophecy:
Listen, and mark the fateful parallel.

I found me, after wanderings on a time
In my Bavarian venturesome far days,
At utter end of the under-earth's dank ways
In a cavern of the mountains of old lime,
Hollowed by waters old.  I stood en-halled,
A thousand paces inward from the sun
And brush about the entrance, whither none
(So said the villagers) had ever crawled.
En-halled mid shadowy wonders in the bleak
And awful silence, vaulted by no stars,
I stood,—my lantern a magnesium wire;
O I remember, even as I speak,
With plangent triumph, how (instead of stars)
Burned there that little point of whitest fire!


Along the shallow pool beneath my foot
Lay antique bones, brown claws and vertebrae
Of bear—the cave-bear, that ancestral brute.
(My City guards in its museum today
The very relics, labelled with the name.)
And near, beneath the long-incrusted lime
(Seen, as through muddy glass, yet seen the same)
I saw charred billets of the olden time—
The cave-men's housing fire and murky flame,
Dead there and cold—how long?  Before me, straight,
Columnar, round, like pipes beyond the nave
(The organ-pipes of some cathedral's fame),
The ranged stalagmites rose; and they were eight—
Waiting the music-master of the cave.

For they were eight; and with a flint I smote
One after other to reverberations,—
And found the octave of the human throat!—
The very scale I found whereby the nations
Have wrought their paeans and their lamentations,
Their symphonies and oratorios:
But what I played was like to none of those;
O what I played with solemn ululations
Was not as music in the skiey places
Of grass and trees: it was a hymn indeed
Of time and mystery and things that none
(However sad and lyrical their faces)
Who have not *wholly* wandered from the sun
Can ever hymn, or, hearing, ever heed.

## XXVII

Under the trees I sat, under the blue
Midsummer morning; under the quiet trees,
Under the twilight, under the little breeze
That scarcely dipped along the hillside dew;
Day after day I sat, to hear some few
Whisperings of the Comforter, and these
My words, with hands clasping my folded knees:
"Knock, and it shall be opened unto you."
My heart, my broken heart, was ready, ready
My utmost soul (that might no longer talk),
Ready for God, still as a leaf grown steady
After the tempest on a shivered stalk:
I made God's test, in all good faith I made it;—
Is there a God?—if so, then he betrayed it.

I made the test in God's own Laboratory
(If sages speak the truth), with each appliance
Perfect in its adjustment; and my Science
Showed no results: there shone no inward glory,
There flooded me no dominant control,
No truth, no peace that passeth understanding;
Until at last, as ship that makes its landing,
I anchored on its native shore my soul,
Knowing this, this: for *me* no Comforter
From Otherwhere, for *me* salvation none,
Save such as by stern action might be won
Among things round me; I said: "It horror were
In *such* a world, were Foresight at the wheel"—
I said: " 'Ich lass den Herrgott aus dem Spiel.' "


I *could* not have beat back my way to life,
Inch after inch, with lacerated shins,
Through thorns and rocks, whilst mocked the Harlequins,
The monstrous midnight shapes of dancing Strife,
Had I still thought, "The Lord is lord of all."—
'T had been too ghastly; but I got good grip
On savior-energy of sportsmanship,
And heard far off Humanity to call
Me to its service. Thus I *would* not die.
And trained the shattered body back to speed,
And back to strength. (Run with me, if you will,
Young athletes— I'll outstrip you to the hill!)—
And trained the mind still forward to the High,
The Keen, the Firm! (And let who should, take heed!)

Ere this, had I abandoned holy house
Of Holy Church, with organ, cross, and book,—
As some dim cob-webbed hunting-lodge forsook
Not yet of bat and wasp, though of the mouse
And eager hound; and now that mystic Union
With Love Divine, as Brahma, Logos, God,—
Preached by the prophets of a World-communion—
Failed me the same, whatever path I trod,
Whatever tree I sate me by. . . . I guess
Ye grieve at such conclusion, saying: "So,
In vain he suffered all the long distress,
For vain his wisdom from his overthrow."—
Spare me (who've been with life) such platitude—
Even I have spelt new meanings for my good,


Like one who solves some curious alphabet
Upon a desert stele. . . . But perhaps
I am too near the tempests of collapse
To tongue their awful intimacies yet
For the articulate world. . . . And if *I* grow
By suffering, where is she? . . . And shall we meet
Somewhere again along the Cosmic Flow,
I and the woman of the winding-sheet?—
All proofs and guesses of ten thousand years
Never have dried one orphaned heart its tears:
I have no proof and but a shadow-guess,
And yet I've never wept. . . . But should we meet,
Would *she* still know me after my distress,
Would *I* still find the words wherewith to greet?

Like one who solves some curious alphabet
On desert stele . . . and then solves a word . . .
Though the God's whispering I never heard,
And though my eyes were cruelly unwet
(Harshly encountering so much to do),
I know how ineradicably absurd
That Man is but a function of the Two,
Physics and Chemistry—that we can spell
By atom and motion (or by twitch and cell)
The ineffable Adventure I've been through. . . .
I know Love, Pain, and Power are spirit-things,
My Act a more than Mine or Now or Near:
One with the Will that suffers, conquers, sings,
*I* was the mystic Voice I could not hear.


## XXVIII

That once the gentle mind of my dead wife
Did love that fiery Roman (dead like her)—
Lucretius and his vast hexameter—
I number with the ironies of life.
That I, who turned his Latian verse to mine
For her, the while she typed each page for me,
Should, in my English, just have reached that line
Fourth from the end of the Book of Death (Book Three),
When Death rode out for her—was that design?—
If so, of God or Devil?—the line which saith,
*"O Mors aeterna*—O eternal Death"—
The last, last letters she fingered key by key! . .
But when, long after, I had wrought the rest,
I said these verses, walking down the west:

## XXIX

### INDIAN SUMMER

(*O Earth-and-Autumn of the Setting Sun,*
*She is not by, to know my task is done!*)

In the brown grasses slanting with the wind,
Lone as a lad whose dog's no longer near,
Lone as a mother whose only child has sinned,
Lone on the loved hill . . . and below me here
The thistle-down in tremulous atmosphere
Along red clusters of the sumach streams;
The shriveled stalks of goldenrod are sere,
And crisp and white their flashing old racemes.
( . . . forever . . . forever . . . forever . . . )
This is the lonely season of the year,
This is the season of our lonely dreams.

(*O Earth-and-Autumn of the setting Sun,*
*She is not by, to know my task is done!*)

The corn-shocks westward on the stubble plain
Show like an Indian village of dead days;
The long smoke trails behind the crawling train,
And floats atop the distant woods ablaze
With orange, crimson, purple. The low haze
Dims the scarped bluffs above the inland sea,
Whose wide and slaty waters in cold glaze
Await yon full-moon of the night-to-be.
( . . . far . . . and far . . . and far . . . )
These are the solemn horizons of man's ways,
These the horizons of solemn thought to me.

(*O Earth-and-Autumn of the Setting Sun,*
*She is not by to know my task is done!*)

And this the hill she visited, as friend;
And this the hill she lingered on, as bride—
Down in the yellow valley is the end:
They laid her . . . in no evening Autumn tide. . . .
Under fresh flowers of that May morn, beside
The queens and cave-women of ancient earth. . . .


This is the hill . . . and over my city's towers,
Across the world from sunset, yonder in air,
Shines, through its scaffoldings, a civic dome
Of pilèd masonry, which shall be ours
To give, completed, to our children there. . . .
And yonder far roof of my abandoned home
Shall house new laughter. . . . Yet I tried. . . . I tried. . . .
And, ever wistful of the doom to come,
I built her many a fire for love . . . for mirth. . . .
(When snows were falling on our oaks outside,
Dear, many a winter fire upon the hearth) . . .
( . . . farewell . . . farewell . . . farewell . . . )
We dare not think too long on those who died,
While still so many yet must come to birth.


*The End*